ENDORSEMENTS

I0051933

I've been in business for myself for over four decades, most of which I've invested in personal development. One lesson that's been consistently reinforced is that before you can effectively lead others, you must first learn to lead yourself. This book captures that truth beautifully. Through authentic storytelling and timeless wisdom, the author reveals that leadership is not about position, power, or comparison—it's about authenticity. There's an old proverb that says, "If he works for you, you work for him." That spirit of mutual respect and responsibility shines through these pages. What I particularly appreciate is how the author disrupts the old paradigm of "follow the leader." Instead, she highlights the traits and attributes of great leaders while reminding us that we all carry the innate capacity to be stellar leaders ourselves. **Leadership ReDEFYned™** invites you to look at leadership through a fresh lens, release limiting ideas, and embrace the idea that authenticity is your greatest strength. If you allow yourself to be coached by Tami, you'll not only rethink what leadership means, you'll discover how to embody it in a way that uplifts yourself and others.

— **Jae M. Rang**,
Catalyst for Positive Change and Inspired Growth

We are all LEADERS, living in a time when we long for GREAT leadership. We need it everywhere ... all at once ... all the time, right now! Tami Chapek provides historical context about leadership in this new book. She offers practical tools, proven techniques, and insightful self-reflection exercises that reveal each person's unique, authentic path to leadership. For such a time as this, her book is vital for raising up a new generation of LEADERS. Bravo!"

— **Kathleen Canova**,
Co-Author Silver Series of Grown-Up Wisdom,
Entrepreneur/Owner The Canova Group, LLC

If you've ever felt that you didn't fit the 'traditional' leadership mold, this book proves that you don't need to. **Leadership reDEFYned™** is a roadmap for unlocking your strengths, leaning into your authenticity, and creating a ripple effect of change in the world around you.

— **Judy O'Beirn**,
Founder and President of Hasmark Publishing International

Leadership reDEFYned™

**DEFY the Ordinary to Unleash
Your Potential**

BY
TAMI CHAPEK

Hasmark
PUBLISHING
INTERNATIONAL

Published by
Hasmark Publishing International
www.hasmarkpublishing.com

Copyright © 2025 Tami Chapek
First Edition

All Rights Reserved.

No part of this book may be reproduced or transmitted in any form or by any means, electronic or mechanical, including photocopying, recording or by any information storage and retrieval system, without written permission from the author, except for the inclusion of brief quotations in a review.

Disclaimer

This book is designed to provide information and motivation to our readers. It is sold with the understanding that the publisher is not engaged to render any type of psychological, legal, or any other kind of professional advice. The content of each article is the sole expression and opinion of its author, and not necessarily that of the publisher. No warranties or guarantees are expressed or implied by the publisher's choice to include any of the content in this volume. Neither the publisher nor the individual author(s) shall be liable for any physical, psycho- logical, emotional, financial, or commercial damages, including, but not limited to, special, incidental, consequential or other damages. Our views and rights are the same: You are responsible for your own choices, actions, and results.

Permission should be addressed in writing to Tami Chapek at tami@weinspirewe.com WeInspireWe® and Leadership Redefyned™ are trademarks of Tami Chapek.

Editor: Debra McCraw Debra.mccraw@gmail.com
Cover Design: Anne Karklins anne@hasmarkpublishing.com
Interior Layout: Amit Dey amit@hasmarkpublishing.com

ISBN 13: 978-1-77482-375-0
ISBN 10: 1-77482-375-6

Hasmark
PUBLISHING
INTERNATIONAL

DEDICATION

To the leader within you, waiting to be unleashed.
May this book be the mirror that reflects your truest self,
for it is there that your greatest leadership resides
—the unique gift the world truly needs.

TABLE OF CONTENTS

PREFACE

I once had a boss who was threatened by me. At least this is how I—and others in my organization— perceived their actions. They were controlling, harsh with feedback, and, as I grew and achieved, I felt like they confined rather than supported me.

I had a choice: to be held back by their fears and need for control, or to lean into who I really was, and could be, as a leader. I chose the latter and focused my energy on stepping up, leading my team forward, and driving for strong business results. Because of that, I won an award—the first one to ever be given to a marketing partner in that organization—and a generous bonus. This was all the validation I needed.

I left the company shortly after, in search of a more supportive leader and greater opportunities to grow my career. This was a pinnacle moment on my journey, and one of many examples demonstrating the value of Leadership reDEFYned™.

The fact that you're reading this book suggests you want to be a good leader and are not willing to accept the conventional standards or the status quo that define leadership today. You are ready to defy the odds and get exactly what you want and deserve. Regardless of where you are in your career, or in your confidence and belief in yourself, know that you are already a leader. And you have the potential to be not just any leader, but a **great** leader!

The term leadership has historically been defined by and of white males, and globally, male leaders still make up the vast majority of C-suite executives today. Leaders have been defined as decisive, assertive, confident, charismatic, strong, professional, and bold. Consider how Julius Caesar, King Henry, Abraham Lincoln, Jack Welch, Jeff Bezos, and Steve Jobs all exhibit those traits.

The problem is that most people in this world are not cisgendered white men. So why do we continue to mold leadership standards and requirements after them? Why do we continue to look at them as the example to emulate leadership success?

Great leadership should not be defined by race, gender, sexual orientation, or any other characterization. It is not about having an exact set of qualities, and it is certainly not about emulating the average leaders that we see today. Leadership needs to evolve along with the workplace and the world. The standards of the past no longer apply. **We must defy those standards and step into a new era—the era of Leadership reDEFYned™.**

Leadership reDEFYned™ is about truly understanding your strengths and gifts and leveraging them to succeed. It is recognizing your limitations and aspirations for growth. It is also about surrounding yourself with people who can balance out different perspectives, strengths, and experiences to advance thinking and exponentially impact results.

Great leadership is not an exact formula, but a lifelong journey of continually learning who you are (your value) and understanding who you want to be (your growth). It's a commitment to tapping into your strengths, motivations, and priorities—and continually seeking opportunities to be a little better than you were the day before.

I want to make something very clear. This book is not an "anti" anything book, and especially not an anti-white male leader book. It's intended to defy the standards stacked against individuals and empower leadership from the beauty, uniqueness, and excellence found within each of us. It's about opening our eyes and definitions to more authentic leadership styles and traits. It's about looking at leadership as a quality, an attitude, and a right, rather than something we are born with or something we can visually see. This book is about defying common leadership standards and ideals, and is something anyone can benefit from, even if you fit into the "current" mold.

This book is about helping you lead in a way that works best for you, as an individual. It's about helping you succeed in a meaningful way. Together, we will embark on a journey to discover the type of leader you already are based on your values, strengths, gifts, and skills, and DEFYne the leader that you want to grow into.

I believe, no, **I know**, that you can positively impact the community around you, whether you realize it or not. You have a gift deep within that allows you to not only be great at the things you do, but also influence, inspire, and deliver exactly what you need for success.

You are a leader today, regardless of who you are and where you are in your professional journey. You are making a difference already, whether you realize it or not. People observe you and learn from you every day. There are people who admire and want to follow you. Now, let's harness that so you can amplify your impact in the most positive and influential way possible: Leadership reDEFYned™.

CHAPTER 1

WHY LEADERSHIP REDEFYNED™
AND WHY NOW?

I was born to be a coach. This might sound dramatic, but I can assure you, looking back on my journey, coaching is in my blood. I have an inherently strong desire and natural ability to listen, support, and motivate others to do and be their best.

I coached my friends and family from a very young age, before I even knew what coaching was. I was a trusted confidante to my mother and sister. I would lend an ear as they talked through situations, asking questions to inspire their actions. My friends frequently called to talk about school, work, and relationships, knowing that I was a good listener and would help them to figure it out. Throughout my career, these skills came to life as I led clients and teams in marketing roles; eventually, these skills evolved, and I became the seasoned leadership development professional I am today.

But before I get too far ahead, let me start a little closer to the beginning. I had always wanted to work in corporate America. I dreamed of wearing power suits and high heels, working from the proverbial corner office, and directing my team toward success, whatever that might be. At the ripe young age of 6, this is what I thought leadership looked like, and I didn't see any barriers to my potential. I didn't understand the limitations that would be put on me as a female or by the paths I would choose for college, jobs, bosses, etc.

By the time I got to college, I was ready to step into something much bigger than my rural Ohio community. I majored in fine arts and business/marketing, allowing me to embark on what I thought was my calling—advertising.

Early in my career, I was blessed with great opportunities, rapid promotions, and a successful track record working in the advertising agency world. When I started managing teams and taking on larger roles, I led through power, subconsciously emulating and mirroring the behaviors of my bosses, all of whom at that time were men. I didn't think much about my approach. I just followed the leader and mimicked what they did. I leaned into my direct personality, strong voice, and results-driven approach to the business.

I took this approach when I was promoted to my first managerial role. I was incredibly excited for the opportunity, but it posed a challenge: I would now be supervising a friend. I didn't think much of the conflict this would raise, but she struggled with how I tried to lead her. I tried to have conversations with her about it, but looking back, I didn't give her the time or space she needed to process. And I certainly didn't give her the opportunity to be open about how she was feeling and figure out what we both needed to succeed. I took her silence as agreement and acceptance, not as her holding back. Rather than being the empathetic leader or coach that I have since learned I am naturally gifted to be, I followed the styles of my bosses and led with an iron fist. My lack of compassion combined with her hurt over the situation, led to difficulties in both our work and personal relationship.

Unfortunately, this approach caused more harm than good. The pendulum had swung too far to one side, and I had left behind my personal values of care, compassion, and empathy, as well as a gift of building interpersonal relationships. I didn't understand the impact of my leadership style. In the end, I was deeply hurt by losing a friend, and I know I hurt her in the process too.

This situation forced me to question how I could be a good leader, or even if I was capable of being one. Being an individual contributor was easy for me, getting great results for my clients was easy, and navigating the stress and dynamic environment of an advertising agency was also relatively easy. I knew the exact impact I was making as the work I did was mine and mine alone. Stepping into management was uncharted territory, and I had no roadmap to success.

I looked around for other leadership examples, but most of the leaders above me were men and relied on traits that I was ultimately getting in trouble for. The few female leaders in the agency also used this same leadership style. I had a big decision to make: Did I continue to try and fit myself into the models I observed, or figure out how to do things my way?

Unfortunately, at the time I opted to continue on the same path and emulate the leaders above me. After all, that was what I thought good leadership looked like. I became bolder, more vocal, and more assertive in my decision-making. This resulted in my already strong voice being perceived as aggressive, my presence being felt as dominating or intimidating, and my need for perfection (aka control), increasing. Without even realizing it, I had moved further away from the best parts of me.

If it worked for them, it should work for me, right? To no surprise, the answer was a resounding no. The feedback I was receiving indicated that this "follow the leader" approach wasn't working, and I was building a dangerous reputation for myself. Luckily, I had the good sense to take the time to reflect, listen, and learn before this path became one I couldn't come back from. While I admired my bosses and what they saw in me, I realized that I had to start picking and choosing what worked for me, not just doing what worked for them.

This approach to leadership didn't work for me because I tried to be someone that I wasn't. I was behaving as I thought I was supposed to, and as I thought leaders *should* act. My behavior did not align with my values and talents, and as a result, I was disconnected from relationships with team members, peers, and, most importantly, myself.

I had forgotten who I was and what my strengths were (besides my ability to achieve business results). I had forgotten about my heart and my desire to give back, to do and be more, to truly listen and have deep connections that go beyond the work itself. I was so driven by results and this pursuit of what I thought good leadership was that I lost sight of what was really important to me—the people. I used to say that relationships make the world go around, and there I was doing the absolute minimum to honor that.

I knew there had to be a better—and hopefully easier—way. I committed to gaining a deeper understanding of leadership principles and learning about other types of leadership models. I became vulnerable with my team, peers, and bosses to ensure that I was both intentional with my leadership growth and my ability to grow in a positive way.

I read as much as I could, listened to podcasts and TED Talks, and took classes. I found a few great mentors and raised my hand at every opportunity that my company offered, and even others that I self-funded.

I reflected on what was good, what worked for me, and what was easy and natural. I thought about what inspired and motivated me. I reflected on what I had in common with my bosses, as well as how I was different. I considered what made (and would make) me a good leader. I leaned into my belief that relationships make the world go around, started to ask more questions and listen more to both what was said and not said, and consider what results really matter.

Naturally, my leadership style changed and evolved. The gifts that I had—empathy, intuition, compassion, a growth-mindset, curiosity, communication skills, expectation setting, strategic planning and execution, and a drive for results—now worked together in harmony versus being in conflict or entirely hidden.

I shifted my focus from business results to the achievements and growth of the individuals around me (which, by the way, led to even better business results). Several of my team members were promoted. I was asked to mentor other women in the agency. I was promoted, given more responsibility, and had a broader reach.

I asked thoughtful questions about perspective, individual desires for growth, motivators, and preferences for feedback. And most importantly, I found that my life was actually easier, not harder. I wasn't fighting an uphill battle every day. I was being me, and I was using my skills and strengths to be a leader. I had reDEFYned my leadership style by leading from within and leading in a way that honored my gifts versus worked against them.

Once things started to click, I felt a duty to pay it forward to other women in my male-dominated workforce. This became my personal mission: to make it easier for the next generation of aspiring leaders, especially women and underrepresented groups who might not have leaders who look or act like them to learn from.

In 2017, I founded WeInspireWe® to bring this mission to life, empowering individuals to be true to themselves and enabling the greatness of their leadership to follow. I believe that the traditional leadership development pathways of mirroring leaders above us are lacking (as I certainly experienced), and when we follow this same approach, we create the same kind of leaders, what I like to call the status quo. This is what we see across most organizations and even in government today.

As a leadership development company, I built WeInspireWe® with the mission of disrupting or defying the status quo, to reDEFYne leadership standards globally, and to create seats at the table for the best leaders, not just the ones that look like or sound like everyone else. We must DEFY the ordinary to unleash the greatest potential. By inspiring one, we inspire many, creating a ripple effect of change and transforming the world into a better place.

Diversity, equity, inclusion, and belonging must continue to be explored and evolve; I am thrilled to see more leaders embrace the idea that authenticity matters more than finding leaders "like us." I love reading articles and studies on the impact of diversity on people, projects, organizations, and businesses as a whole. I love seeing the number of diverse leaders rising year over year as we work to embrace our differences as a strength, not a detriment.

But we still have so far to go.

So back to the original question: why Leadership reDEFYned™ and why now?

Leadership reDEFYned™ uses your competitive advantage— your strengths, talents, experience, and perspective—to create positive movement. It's an opportunity to DEFY the current standards and bring innovation through new perspectives and approaches, leading to better results.

As the world and the workplace evolve, so must our approach to leadership. My experience of learning to lead authentically and truly step into great leadership is not unique. I've heard similar stories from other leaders, and I've seen it happen when coaching others. The more you align your leadership style to your values, strengths, and gifts, the more successful you will be.

Read that again: The more you align your leadership style to your values, strengths, and gifts, the more successful you will be.

This holds true in our professional *and* personal lives. The more you know yourself, the more you can lean into those strengths, the greater your impact, and most importantly, the greater your happiness. (And by the way, when we are happier, the people around us are happier too!)

We must have a sense of urgency and a heightened priority to shifting the status quo and approaches to leadership. We can no longer wait for someone else to create a better world for us. It's on us, *every single one of us*, to create a new and better future. The time to act is now, the time to shift our leadership perspective and reDEFYne leadership is now, and the time to be better is right now. We must grab the proverbial bull by the horns and take action. If not for our own betterment, for the people around us and the future generations to come.

With that, I invite you to join me on this path to **Leadership reDEFYned™.** It isn't always easy—it takes effort and practice—but my intent is to make the path to great leadership more simplified, far more rewarding, and far more successful than traditional leadership models.

CHAPTER 2

WHAT IS A LEADER, REALLY?

If I asked 100 people what defines being a leader, 99 would likely say that it's about reaching a certain professional level in a position of authority. Many people associate leadership with a title, management responsibility, a large salary, or even a certain look that traditional leaders are perceived to have; the list goes on and on. We tend to look for these symbols and identifiers to label someone as a leader. This label feeds into the amount of respect we both consciously and subconsciously give to someone.

Many of us aspire to associate leadership with our own name and work hard to attain it. Some people become leaders and view this as the pinnacle, the culmination of their journey. But the philosophy behind Leadership reDEFYned™ is that as you embrace being a leader, you are continually learning and growing into the best possible leader, making the concerted effort to be one little bit better today than you were the day before.

One of the reasons that I felt the need to control when and how things were getting done as a new manager was because I felt it was my reputation on the line. As an individual contributor, my work spoke for itself; when something was good, it was a direct reflection of my abilities. But when I thought about how people would measure my success as a leader, I thought they would look at accomplishments only (e.g., what my team did), not at my leadership style (e.g., how I motivated and inspired others). Shifting my perspective from focusing on business results to focusing on people allowed me and my team to grow and evolve.

Leadership is a process, not a position.
—John C. Mitchell

This growth and evolution process is extremely healthy and an ongoing investment that we should all be making in ourselves. It's a process I started when I decided to flip the script about what leadership meant to me; a process that continues today. Rather than waiting until you are seen as a leader, until you get that leadership title, or until you feel like you've been deemed as a leader, I challenge you to reDEFYne your leadership today and embrace it as your leadership journey.

Everyone is a leader.

Let me say that again. Everyone is a leader, regardless of title or tenure, age or gender, sexual orientation, religion, personality type, and more.

But before that feels like a controversial statement, let's break down what a leader really is:

lead·er·ship

/lē-dər-ship/

noun

- the position or function of a leader, <u>a person who guides or directs</u> a group: *He managed to maintain his leadership of the party despite heavy opposition.*
- <u>ability to lead</u>: *As early as sixth grade, she displayed remarkable leadership potential.*
- <u>an act or instance of leading; guidance; direction</u>: *They prospered under his strong leadership.*
- the leaders of a group: *The union leadership agreed to arbitrate.*

to lead

/lēd/

verb (used with object), led, lead·ing.

- <u>to go before or with to show the way</u>; conduct or escort: *to lead a group on a cross-country hike.*
- to <u>conduct</u> by holding and guiding: *to lead a horse by a rope.*

verb (used without object), led, lead·ing.

- <u>to act as a guide; show the way</u>: *You lead, and we'll follow.*
- to afford passage to a place: *That path leads directly to the house.*

noun

- the first or foremost place; position in advance of others: He took the lead in the race.
- the extent of such an advance position: He had a lead of four lengths.

While you will find multitudes of definitions on leadership, leading, or to lead, I argue that the basic concept is this:

Leadership is forward movement.

Leadership is moving oneself, someone, or something forward.

It is moving a project or an initiative forward; it is moving an individual or a group forward. It is momentum, progress, and action in the purest form; leadership is motivation, inspiration, and adaptation.

Leadership is not just a work thing. Every day, leaders move their families, friends, households, and communities forward.

In this reDEFYned definition of leadership as moving forward, everyone in this world has the ability to lead, should they choose to embrace that right and take control of their future.

While everyone is capable of leading, not everyone chooses to take on a leader role. Unfortunately, even when we want to take on the role of a leader, most of us don't proactively embrace it. We tend to wait until we have been given permission to lead; yet waiting for the title or authority could be detrimental to your long-term potential. On the flip side, just because you have been designated as a leader doesn't automatically make you a good (or great) one.

What Makes a Great Leader?

Google "qualities of leaders" and you'll get results that read "Top 10 Qualities of a Leader", or "8 Aspects of Great Leadership", or "21 Attributes of Leadership", and so on. So, who is to say what great leadership is?

Here's a sampling of the many qualities of leaders, according to my extremely scientific research (aka Google search results, pages 1 and 2).

Although these words *describe* leadership, none of these words fully *define* leadership. It's impossible to say what makes someone a leader, a good leader, or even a great leader. These qualities also don't appear in every leader. For a leader to use any of these qualities effectively, they must be authentic to them. The more you are forced to exhibit qualities and leadership approaches that don't align with your true self, the more difficult it is to become a good or great leader.

Rather than forcing yourself to be a certain way or do something that doesn't feel right, I challenge you to embrace what is core to who *you* are. Remember, Leadership reDEFYned™ is moving (self, others, things) forward while tapping into your authenticity, and staying true to your gifts and strengths, with a growth mindset.

Despite this laundry list of qualities, there is a common thread that holds true when considering good leadership. The basis of it is simply the ability to be effective, to influence, and to inspire others in a positive and meaningful way.

I call these the three principles of leadership:

- **Principle 1:** Be Effective
- **Principle 2:** Influence Others
- **Principle 3:** Inspire Greatness

Tom Peters, an expert in business management practices, has said that *good leadership is not about creating followers or having authority; it's about creating more leaders.* Good leaders don't force their vision onto others, demand followers, or control situations. Good leaders empower others in a positive and meaningful way so they can think, act, and continually grow who they are as individuals. Good leaders will influence, inspire, and create effective movement.

> *Leaders don't create followers,*
> *they create more leaders.*
> *—Tom Peters*

Leadership reDEFYned™ offers a pathway from good to great, by blending your authenticity (i.e., the best version of you) with the three principles of leadership. This combination empowers leaders to evolve from average to exceptional.

This book is dedicated to guiding you through how to become that *great* leader.

LEADERSHIP
REDEFYNED

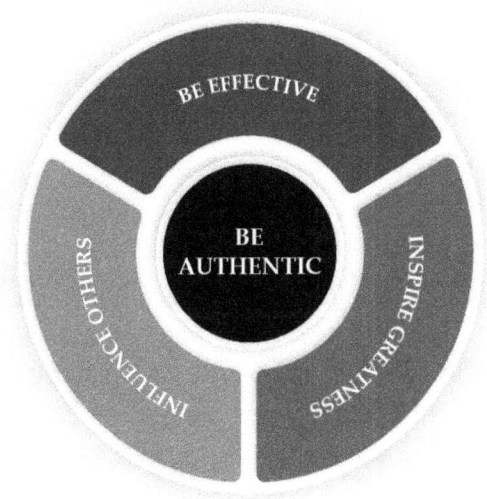

Spoiler alert! Here are some of the things we'll work on together:

1. **Authentic leadership: Know and be yourself.** *To thine own self be true.* The more you can identify, embrace, and leverage your gifts, strengths, and values, the greater the leader you will be. And equally so, the more that you can honor those differences in yourself and others, the more you will empower diversity, create opportunities, and drive innovation.

2. **Efficacy: Know and do your stuff well.** Gain credibility by knowing the ins and outs of your responsibilities and commitments—and following through on what you say you are going to do. Show up on time, focus on your priorities, and deliver strong results.

3. **Influence: Know your audience.** To be a great leader, you must know what motivates others, what's important to them, and what they need to be successful. This changes based on who you're leading, whether it's family, friends, peers, employees, or cross-functional partners. Adjusting accordingly demonstrates that you care, proves you are in this together, and enables you to influence action for greater impact.

4. **Inspire: Know how to motivate.** It's one thing to influence others to action, but to do it with greater energy will ultimately lead to better results. Being confident in yourself, your vision, and your abilities will inspire others to want to listen, follow, and grow alongside you. This will enable you to motivate with deeper meaning and connection to the work, resulting in optimized outcomes versus just movement.

Understand that being a great leader is a process, one that you are highly capable of. Rather than waiting for the right time, start building your leadership muscles today. **Decide what kind of leader you want to be and take the steps to grow into that leader. Begin your path toward Leadership reDEFYned™ now.**

CHAPTER 3

HOW DID WE GET IT SO WRONG?

As a young leader, I thought that my job was to make sure the work got done. I had a one-track mind about output and results. Here's the task: do it exactly this way, check the box, move on to the next thing. I was a machine and treated my team members like they were machines. Without thought for the human being behind the work, I lasered in on the projects, the deadlines, and the processes, and unfortunately, created a difficult work environment for the people around me.

I didn't intend to, and I certainly didn't realize I was doing it. I acted based on the information in front of me, how I was treated by my superiors, and how I was rewarded for my efforts. I was like Pavlov's dog—do the task, get a treat. Get the work done and get a pat on the back. Rinse and repeat.

But that was wrong in so many ways. My team members certainly didn't thrive, our relationships suffered, and—with my eyes on the work only—I lost sight of what truly mattered.

This obviously wasn't successful. How did I end up here? I'm not the only one who has taken this journey; it is the premise of most micromanagers and bad leaders in the world. I needed to take a step back and reset.

I believe that everyone can benefit from taking a step back to reflect and reset.

Now, let's examine the history of leadership. This will provide important context to Leadership reDEFYned™ and your pathway to great leadership. As you would expect, leadership theory and principles have evolved over time as society has progressed. While there is a laundry list of theories, they basically started out with a set of rules around gender that evolved into personality traits. These traits slowly progressed into new personality traits more aligned with the generational needs of today.

Era	Period	Theory	Description
Personality	Great Man, 1841, 1869, 1927	Great Man	
Trait	**1840s**	**Great Man**	**Focus on natural born leaders**
Trait	Trait, 1927	Trait Theory	
Trait	**1930s-1940s**	**Trait**	**Focus on identifying traits and characteristics of effective leaders**
Influence	Power Relations Period, 1956, 1959	Five Bases of Power Approach	Legitimate power, reward power, coercive power, expert power
Influence	Persuasion Period, 1928	Leader Dominance Approach	
Behavioral	**1940s-1950s**	**Behavioral**	**Focus on the actions and skills of leaders**
Behavior	Early Behavior Period, 1960	Reinforced Change Theory	
Behavior	Early Behavior Period, 1955	Ohio State Studies	
Behavior	Early Behavior Period, 1961	Michigan State Studies	
Behavior	Late Behavior Period, 1964	Managerial Grid Model	
Behavior	Late Behavior Period, 1966	Four-Factor Theory	
Behavior	Late Behavior Period, 1976	Action Theory of Leadership	
Behavior	Late Behavior Period, 1966	Theory X and Y	
Situational	**1960s**	**Contingent and Situational**	**Focus on leaders adapting their style taking into account the environment**
Situation	Environment Period, 1943	Environment Approach	
Situation	Environment Period, 1978	Open-Systems Model	
Situation	Social Status Period, 1959	Role Attainment Theory	
Situation	Social Status Period, 1959	Leader Role Theory	

Situation	Sociotechnical Period, 1951	Sociotechnical Systems	
Contingency	1964	Contingency Theory	
Contingency	1971	Path-Goal Theory	
Contingency	1977	Situational Theory	
Contingency	1971, 1989	Multiple Linkage Model	
Contingency	1973, 1988	Normative Theory	
Transactional	Exchange Period, 1973	Vertical Dyad Linkage/Leader Member Exchange	
Transactional	Exchange Period, 1973	Reciprocal Influence Approach	
Transactional	Exchange Period, 1958	Emergent Leadership	
Transactional	Role Development Period, 1979, 1970	Social Exchange Theory	
Transactional	Role Development Period, 1973	Role Making Model	
New leadership	**1990s**	**Transactional**	**Focus on leadership as a cost-benefit exchange**
Anti-Leadership Era	Ambiguity Period, 1977	Attribution Approach	
Anti-Leadership Era	Substitute Period, 1978	Leadership Substitute Theory	
Culture Era	1981	McKinsey 7-S Framework	
Culture Era	1978	Theory Z	
Culture Era	1982	In Search of Excellence Approach	
Culture Era	1985	Schein	
Culture Era	1987	Self-Leadership	
Transformational Era	**Charisma Period, 1977**	**Charismatic Theory**	**Focus on an inspirational style pushing followers to higher and higher levels of achievement**
Transformational Era	Charisma Period, 1978	Transforming Leadership Theory	
Transformational Era	Self-Fulfilling Prophecy Period, 1989, 1984	SFP Leader Theory	
Transformational Era	1985	Performance Beyond Expectations Approach	
New leadership	1990s	Transformational	
New leadership	2000s	Shared	
New leadership	2000s	Collaborative	
New leadership	2000s	Collective	
New leadership	2000s	Servant	
New leadership	2000s	Inclusive	
New leadership	2000s	Complexity	

Source: https://www.semanticscholar.org/paper/Evolution-of-Leadership-Theory-King/7aa50ad4187a85403b60fadaab20ec65d31952ff

The history of the world is but the
biography of great men.
— Thomas Carlyle

The Great Man and Trait Leadership Theories

For centuries, society has ascribed to the belief that being a leader is a God-given right and title. Going as far back as we can in history, men have often taken on the role of leader and owned it. In the 1800s, The Great Man Theory of leadership became a well-known concept and was founded on the belief that the best leaders are born, not made. Examples include Abraham Lincoln, Alexander the Great, and Napolean. Historian Thomas Carlyle helped to popularize this theory when he said, "The history of the world is but the biography of great men."

Great Man leadership qualities: Charisma, intelligence, political savviness, judgment, courage, aggressiveness, persuasion, intuition, and wisdom.

As The Great Man Theory evolved into the Trait Theory, leaders were no longer divinely selected, but they were people (let's be honest, mostly men) who inherently exhibited specific traits and qualities. This shift took hold in the mid-1800s and continued into and beyond the 1970s.

Trait Theory leadership qualities: Competitiveness, achievement, orientation, self-assuredness, dominance, agreeableness, conscientiousness, emotional stability, intelligence, physical energy, and extraversion

Transformational Leadership Theory

While there are many small steps between, Transformational Leadership theory stands out as the next big shift in leadership theory and aligns with the cultural evolution happening in the 1960s and 1970s, including activism for women, people of color, and gay rights. This theory recognizes that connections and relationships are critical to successful leadership. James MacGregor Burns, who helped develop the theory, stated, "Leaders and followers make each other to advance to a higher level of morale and motivation."

Transformational leaders are in a state of constant growth with a strong desire for everyone they associate with to fulfill their greatest potential. This causes a ripple effect, where one can influence many to create positive, lasting change. Unlike the Great Man and Trait theories, it is not limited to birthright or gender.

Over time, additional criteria or principles were considered:

- **Idealized influence:** Use charisma, curiosity, and effective messaging (simple and tactful)
- **Inspirational motivation:** Set, commit, and positively motivate others toward a specific vision or purpose
- **Intellectual stimulation:** Promote collaboration through innovative, out-of-the-box thinking and problem-solving skills
- **Individual consideration:** Recognize and value individuals' motivations, desires, and needs

Transformational leadership qualities: Problem-solver, innovative, curious, organized, creative, nurturing, people-oriented, respected and respectful, responsible, accountable, coach, motivator, influenced by example, optimized based on individual needs

While there are many other leadership theories, the Great Man, Trait, and Transformational Leadership theories have made the biggest impact on how leadership is understood today. Ask other leaders, colleagues, family, and friends how they describe leadership, and you'll probably find a cross-section of these theories.

Great Man and Trait Theory	Transformational Leadership Theory
• Drive	• Problem-solver
• Task-oriented	• Innovative and curious
• Vigor / persistence	• Optimize based on individual needs
• Results / goals-oriented	• Creative
• Risk-taker	• Team-player / people-oriented
• Take charge	• Nurturing
• Fixer / doer	• Respected / respectful
• Lead to success	• Coach
• Authority	• Motivator
• Influence through demand	• Responsible and accountable
	• Influence by example

Why is This so Wrong?

When it comes to expanding our view of who can be a leader, these theories show progress and growth, but we still have far to go. All of these theories focus on specific characteristics or qualities. From being a man born to greatness, to strong, assertive qualities traditionally recognized as masculine traits, to a focus on continual growth and development (traditionally recognized as feminine qualities). We continue to tell people that they have to learn how to have these particular traits to be a leader, instead of leaning into their natural gifts and qualities.

This focus on learned behavior is not exclusive to leadership. From day one of life, we emulate the behavior of those around us. Children learn through observation and modeling, but it's not only children who learn this way—all humans do! We are hardwired to keep growing, evolving, learning, and advancing. We are also hardwired to take the path of least resistance (and least amount of consciousness), which is observation and modeling.

As children subconsciously observe and model adult behavior, they see what leadership looks like through parents, teachers, pop culture, politicians, and more. The leaders or bosses many of us saw in our childhood were white cisgendered men. While there has been an intentional effort to bring more diversity into leadership roles, no one can argue that this demographic still holds the majority of leadership roles and is often presumed to be the "head of," whether they have that title or not.

How Many CEOs or C-suite Leaders are Men?

In its 2023 *Women in the Workplace* report, McKinsey and Company found that 72% of the C-suite in North America was comprised of men. The percentage of women in leadership roles continues to improve, but there's still work to be done. When you see that entry-level roles are held by 48% women, but the C-suite is only 28%, you can't help but ask why.

Looking at women of color, the percentages are even smaller, making up 18% of entry-level roles, but only 6% of the C-suite. The percentage of men of color in entry-level roles versus in the C-suite is not drastically different (18% versus 15%), however, the 15% of men of color is significantly smaller than the 57% of white men in the C-suite.

Women's representation saw modest gains throughout the corporate pipeline, but women of color remain underrepresented.

Representation in corporate role, by gender and race, 2023, % of employees (n = 276)

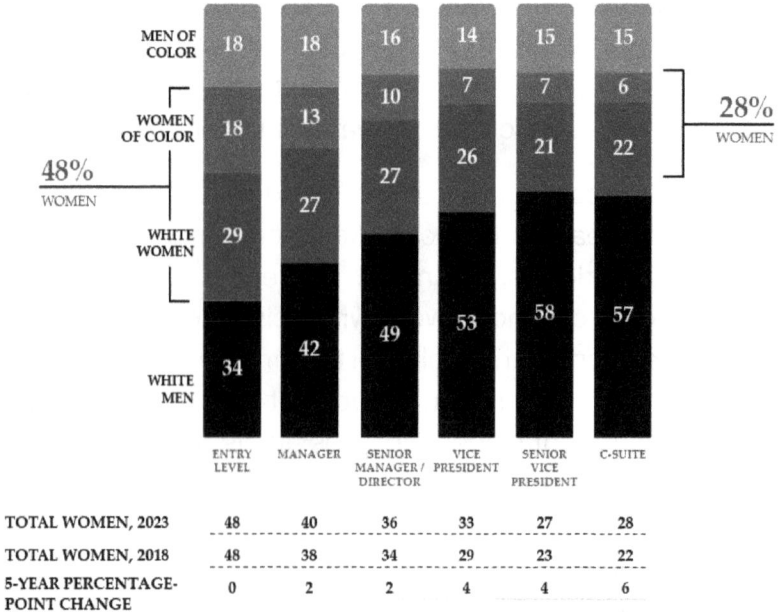

	ENTRY LEVEL	MANAGER	SENIOR MANAGER / DIRECTOR	VICE PRESIDENT	SENIOR VICE PRESIDENT	C-SUITE
MEN OF COLOR	18	18	16	14	15	15
WOMEN OF COLOR	18	13	10	7	7	6
WHITE WOMEN	29	27	27	26	21	22
WHITE MEN	34	42	49	53	58	57

48% WOMEN

28% WOMEN

	ENTRY LEVEL	MANAGER	SENIOR MANAGER / DIRECTOR	VICE PRESIDENT	SENIOR VICE PRESIDENT	C-SUITE
TOTAL WOMEN, 2023	48	40	36	33	27	28
TOTAL WOMEN, 2018	48	38	34	29	23	22
5-YEAR PERCENTAGE-POINT CHANGE	0	2	2	4	4	6

MCKINSEY & COMPANY (2024).
WOMEN IN THE WORKPLACE 2023.

There is a saying, *you can't be what you can't see.* As illustrated in the McKinsey data, white women, women of color, and men of color make up less than half of the C-suite. When junior staff, or even students and children, don't see people who look like them in leadership positions, they struggle to believe it's even an option for them, and far fewer doors are opened to them due to a lack of representation at all levels.

Look back to the leadership theories described earlier: if people don't think they have the defined traits of a leader, if they don't think they can learn to act in a specific way, and if they don't have opportunities or recognition to be leaders, they won't inherently know they can become leaders and will subconsciously limit their own potential. This is aside from the blatant discrimination that happens every day.

Historically, white cisgendered men (as a group) have had the support, the networks, and the champions to propel them to leadership, while other groups have not. White men don't face systemic racism and discrimination. White men are not typically put in a position where they have to choose between pursuing their professional growth or navigating the competing priorities of work and being a primary caregiver. White men are not typically deemed as aggressive or angry simply because of how they express their opinions in the workplace. White cisgendered men don't have to hide parts of their identity to fit the mold.

These privileges have enabled the continued success of white men as leaders and has, in effect, held everyone else back. Let me state again here that this is *not* an anti-white cisgendered male book, but the systems have historically been stacked against everyone else—sometimes intentionally, sometimes not.

How Many are White Men?

Sure, the men vs. women demographics are broad, so let's break it down even further. If we lump men into two categories: white men and men of color, and women into two categories: white women and women of color, we see that there is still a significant discrepancy in leadership outside of white men, with a whopping 57% still holding leadership roles in corporations and ultimately still exemplifying the standard image of leadership.

But by lumping all men of color and all women of color in a single group, we are still limiting the ability to be what you can see. The numbers here are even more astounding when looking at the distribution of white versus black, Latino, or Asian: 79% of the C-suite is white, whether men or women.

Add another layer, sexual orientation. Gender norms don't necessarily apply in the LGBTQ+ community, therefore creating another challenge in how leadership is seen, and in how underrepresented groups can become the kind of leaders they want to be.

You Can't Be What You Can't See

When the "ideal view" of leadership is generally seen as white male, and you mostly see white male leaders, it is extremely difficult for someone who is not that to envision themselves achieving that goal. It sets individuals up for failure when the unwritten rules and accepted standards are created based on something that they aren't. Navigating professional and personal life in an inauthentic way is like trying to force a square peg into a round hole.

Rather than continue trying to conform to these unrealistic standards, it's time to change the way that leaders are evaluated. We must make a path where uniqueness empowers the ability to lead, not where it separates us and takes us further away from being a leader. This is what Leadership reDEFYned™ is all about.

Apart from advancing the individual's ability to lead, Leadership reDEFYned™ is about dismantling systemic racism and discrimination, cultivating role models, champions, and mentors specifically for women, for people of color, for the LGBTQIA+ community, for people from low-income families and rural areas, and for all other groups that are underrepresented in leadership.

As you grow in your leadership journey, consider how you can lift others up creating a leadership ripple effect. You can be a great leader—and you can inspire great leaders too!

CHAPTER 4

AUTHENTICITY STARTS WITH AWARENESS

Leadership reDEFYned™ is the art of discovering who you are (and who you want to be) so that you can effectively lead others in great ways. Understanding what you excel at and what motivates and drives you will position you to lead from an authentic and powerful place. It also helps you identify people who complement, challenge, or enhance your perspective.

> *Authenticity is the daily practice of letting go*
> *of who we think we're supposed to be and*
> *embracing who we are.*
> *— Brene Brown*

As an example, one of my greatest strengths is listening, both to what *is* being said and what is *not* being said. This talent was instrumental in my success as a strategist and account leader in advertising and is core to my leadership coaching role today. This strength plays into my relationships and my ability to be a great friend, sister, daughter, and partner. I know that I have the gift of collecting insights and supporting others to move forward. I'm great at collecting insights about myself and my business, but I also know that I am not always the best at taking those insights and turning them into action, especially within my business.

I recognize this as an area of improvement, so I've found partners who can help me get there. Liz is my collaborator and creative problem solver. She challenges my thinking and helps me to build upon the insights I've collected. She asks great questions that open up my perspective and consider new possibilities. Sarah helps me get unstuck; she is decisive and direct and knows how to turn ideas into results-driven action. She inspires quick action and encourages a "fast failure" mindset rather than procrastination or over-analyzing. These amazing partners offer me perspective, guidance, and direction; they help me prioritize ideas and strategize on how to bring them to life; they balance out my strengths and help me get out of my own way.

I've had to learn more about myself and understand what works and what doesn't. I've had to have some honest conversations with myself and gather feedback from people who have experienced my leadership in various roles, both professional and personal. This deep dive and inventory process is where Leadership reDEFYned™ starts—with deep self-reflection. First, understanding; second, leaning into your gifts and talents; and third, having an eye for continual growth and self-improvement. Leadership reDEFYned™ is knowing the best parts of yourself and how you want to grow and intentionally focusing on how you (alone) can best move forward.

What is Your Competitive Advantage?

It's fascinating how few people truly understand who they are deep down, what makes them tick, or what makes them special and unique. All too often, people downplay their own gifts and talents with the assumption that everyone else has the same ones; that what we have and who we are isn't unique but rather a commodity. Similar to how we can forget how we appear to a stranger, we also forget how others see our skills, talents, and gifts—or our competitive advantage.

*You are so used to your features, you don't know
how beautiful you look to a stranger.*
— Unknown

I can remember working on my résumé several years ago, trying to decide what to include in it. I struggled to come up with language that described my skills and achievements that felt worthy. I felt like I was bragging and was uncomfortable with putting pen to paper. I wound up hiring a résumé writer because I knew I was missing something. After he interviewed me, what he came back with blew me away. The language he used to describe me and my skills, qualities, and achievements was powerful. It was then, for the first time, that I realized I not only had a lot to offer, but also a unique blend of experiences and skills that was mine and mine alone.

You have that power, too. I work with clients every day who undervalue what they have to offer. While our attributes and independent experiences may be similar to others in some capacity, the combination of our values, skills, experiences, worldview, etc. is unique to you and you alone. That is what makes every individual special, and that is something powerful. To paraphrase the great baseball player Satchel Paige, you may have been born average, but you don't have to be common.

From Self-Reflection to Self-Awareness

As you further explore your own uniqueness and your approach to being a great leader, you have to tune into what works for you and what doesn't. Self-awareness is a tricky concept, though, because you can *feel* very self-aware but still have massive blind spots in how you present yourself or what you understand about yourself.

Self-awareness involves an honest assessment of yourself, the good and the not-so-good. To be truly self-aware, you must be in tune with your skills, unique qualities, and areas of opportunity. Some people are naturally in tune with themselves and can tap into this intuition, but many of us need outside support to reach this level of authenticity. Lack of self-awareness can lead to being out of touch with reality and underdelivering. Too much self-awareness without a balanced perspective can cause insecurity or overconfidence.

Part of this exploration is not just a broad awareness of our qualities, skills, and experiences, but is also the realization that there is a deep interconnectivity between our thoughts, feelings, and actions. To further explain: every thought that you have connects to a feeling or emotion that connects to an action (or inaction) you take. The more you are in tune with your thoughts, feelings, and actions, the more self-awareness you have, especially for situational leadership skills. A deep level of self-awareness involves intentionally identifying these connections and understanding how they influence your behavior. (Note: This is core to cognitive behavioral therapy if you'd like to further understand these connections.)

Example 1

- Thought: I wish I didn't have to do this presentation.
- Feeling: I am nervous that I will make a fool of myself.
- Action: I'm procrastinating on working on the presentation.

Example 2

- Thought: It's Monday, so I should go to the gym today.
- Feeling: I know I feel good when I go to the gym.
- Action: I went to the gym and am having a good workout.

Being self-aware helps you understand what's working and what isn't, both at the macro and micro levels. It gives you power in how you show up every day, and it helps you align your actions with your values, providing for more harmony and less conflict in your life.

Psychologists Shelley Duval and Robert Wicklund define self-awareness as "...the ability to focus on yourself and how your actions, thoughts, or emotions do or don't align with your internal standards. If you're highly self-aware, you can objectively evaluate yourself, manage your emotions, align your behavior with your values, and understand correctly how others perceive you... Developing self-awareness is important because it allows leaders to assess their growth and effectiveness and change course when necessary."

Self-awareness is crucial and offers us many benefits, including:

- Power to impact outcomes
- Increased decision-making skills
- Improved self-confidence
- Clear and intentional communication
- Ability to understand multiple perspectives
- Decreased limiting beliefs, assumptions, or biases
- Improved relationships
- Improved self-regulation (better manage how we show up)
- Decreased stress
- Increased satisfaction

Drs. Duval and Wicklund break down self-awareness into two categories.

Public self-awareness is the understanding of how you show up, appear to, or are perceived by others.

- **Upside:** The ability to self-regulate so you are accepted and understood by those around you.
- **Downside:** You can worry too much about what others think and shift your approach to be what you think you *should* be versus what you really are.
- **Example**: You have to deliver difficult news to your team. You spend extra time working through the talking points and positioning, thinking about what this news means to them. You also do a breathing exercise before the meeting to ensure you're calm and compassionate.

Private self-awareness is the ability to know yourself and reflect on your thoughts, feelings, and actions.

- **Upside:** You are very in tune with yourself and understand what works for you and what doesn't.
- **Downside:** You may overcompensate or live in a state of avoidance to protect yourself from feeling uncomfortable.
- **Example**: You recognize that you're in a bad mood. You take a beat to understand why and determine how much you want this mood to impact your day.

When broken into these two categories, self-awareness aligns with Jean Greaves and Travis Bradberry's definition of emotional intelligence, as presented in their book *Emotional Intelligence 2.0*. Emotional intelligence is the balance between self-awareness, social awareness, and the ability to regulate your approach to both.

As I noted earlier, I had a hard time when I was first given the title of a leader. (I say it that way because I don't know that I was truly leading.) I behaved as I thought I was supposed to. I lacked private self-awareness of the disconnect between my values and my actions. I also lacked public self-awareness, as I had no idea the harm I was causing others.

- **Thought:** The work must be done to the highest standards possible.
- **Feeling:** I feel pressure to deliver.
- **Action:** I micromanage every task, project, and outcome.

As I became more self-aware—both publicly and privately—I realized that I was hurting my success, and even worse, I was hurting the people around me. So, I had to pivot with this new awareness and shift to a new approach.

- **New thought:** The work will be done to the highest possible standards when people are motivated and cared for.
- **New feeling:** I feel compassion and empathy for those around me.
- **New action:** I empower individuals to do their best work, there way, thus growing the overall business.

Regardless of categories and definitions, the more self-aware you are, the more choice you have as a leader in how you help to move others forward. The more in tune you are with your thoughts, feelings, and actions, the greater your ability to connect with what works for you and navigate away from what doesn't.

Gaining Self-Awareness is the First Step to Leadership reDEFYned™

Self-awareness gives you the opportunity to fully understand your strengths, passions, desires, skills, perspective, expertise, and interests. It helps you understand all the things you are good at. It helps you learn which of these will fill you up and which will deplete you. It helps you understand how you might want to grow in the future, how to be vulnerable and ask for help, and when to bow out of certain situations.

Self-awareness can also help you battle imposter syndrome. Having healthy self-awareness will give you the confidence to know that you do belong in leadership positions. You have the talent and expertise to lead and to address all the challenges that come with being a leader.

The More You Know, Right?

Yes, knowledge is power, and power is knowledge. And this kind of knowledge—knowledge about yourself, i.e., self-awareness – is the most powerful because it gives you choice in how you lead.

You gotta know when to hold 'em
know when to fold'em
know when to walk away
know when to run
— Don Schlitz (made famous by Kenny Rogers)

Awareness Enables Choice

It allows you to make decisions and take action (or inaction) influenced by your natural instincts, your ability to serve others, your core values, and more. The good stuff.

It allows you to know when to be decisive, when to collaborate, and when to seek help.

Awareness gives you the ability to say, "Does this serve me?" or "Does this make a positive or a negative impact?" or "Is this really what I want to be doing right now?" Awareness is 50% of the equation, choice is the other 50%.

Self-Awareness Leads to Authenticity

Often, people hear the word *authentic* and start to zone out. Unfortunately, the word is overused and often misunderstood. In fact, it was deemed the word of the year in 2023!

---

authentic

au·then·tic ə-'then-tik

1: not false or imitation: real, actual
an authentic cockney accent

2: true to one's own personality, spirit, or character
is sincere and authentic with no pretensions

3a: worthy of acceptance or belief as conforming to or based on fact *paints an authentic picture of our society*
3b: conforming to an original so as to reproduce essential features
an authentic reproduction of a colonial farmhouse
3c: made or done the same way as an original
authentic Mexican fare

4a of a church mode: ranging upward from the keynote
4b of a cadence: progressing from the dominant chord to the tonic

---

Authenticity is about being real. It's not false or imitation; it's true character and personality. It's you at your core—or the essence of you.

Self-awareness allows you to identify what makes you uniquely you, and to be authentic and true to that. Being authentic to yourself is an easier, more satisfying, and more impactful way to live. Being authentic is choosing to lean into your gifts, talents, and strengths.

I'll also caveat that authenticity should be wrapped around positive intent and connected to a growth mindset. Some people may use authenticity as a crutch or excuse for toxic behavior, saying, "I am who I am." Being authentic and true to who you are does not give you permission to be cruel or abrasive, or to put your needs over everyone else's. Being resistant to feedback or stagnant in your growth does not align with true authenticity.

Being authentic is about understanding yourself, understanding the impact you want to make on the world, and taking thoughtful steps in that direction. It means that you know who you are, and you honor that with a dialed approach.

A dialed approach is the idea that you are still authentic and true to who you are, but you may lean into your decision-making skills more or less in a given situation, or into your listening skills more or less in a given situation, etc. For example, in some settings, you can honor your authenticity and dial up your directness to drive home a meaningful point, while in other situations, you will need to dial down that directness and dial up curiosity to allow others to feel heard. Another example might be that you need to dial up your level of executive presence and dial down your casual tone, or vice versa, to have the most meaningful impact on the environment around you.

In these instances, you are not changing who you are but being strategic and selective in how much you tap into each component of your uniqueness to best serve the situation and the people around you. You are not changing who you are, but you're consciously choosing what strength or skill to tap into to achieve the greatest results This is emotional intelligence at its finest, which takes time and practice.

You Be YOU

The more you understand your competitive advantage (awareness) and the more you can embrace the dial (choice), the greater impact you will make (intentional leadership).

Awareness + Choice = *Intentional* Leadership

Self-awareness gives you the ability to be more thoughtful and understand what you want and what you need. It also gives you the ability to understand where you can add value, how you might want to grow, and how you might want to lean on others. It teaches you about your competitive advantage and where that advantage is best used.

To be yourself in a world that is constantly trying to make you something else is the greatest accomplishment.
— Ralph Waldo Emerson

These skills open the door for you to be selective and intentional in how you show up every day, how you lead yourself, and ultimately how you lead others. You have a choice in those things. And the more aware you are, the more choices you have. The more you are in tune with your thoughts, your feelings, and your actions, the more you can shift or adjust to lead to a meaningful outcome.

This combination of awareness and choice adds up to the *you that you are today*.

Let me repeat that.

Knowing what's what is first; choosing what to do with it is second. The combination of those two things is authenticity, which is what gives you the ability to lead from a place of intention versus reaction. Leading with intention is powerful because you are able to put your choice into action, versus just a thought or a feeling that you have buried within. Intentional leadership is the core of leadership reDEFYned™.

CHAPTER 5

INTENTIONAL LEADERSHIP FOR TODAY AND TOMORROW

L et's dig into that equation:

Awareness + Choice = *Intentional* Leadership

You can be self-aware and recognize what you bring to the table, but to truly reDEFYne leadership, you need to choose to leverage your qualities to be more effective, more influential, and more inspirational. Let's talk about choice and what it really means for your ability to lead with intention.

Choice is a big word that is often underplayed and misunderstood. Believe it or not, in life you always have a choice. All choices have consequences, some known and realized, and some unknown or not considered. But you have a choice, nonetheless. It may not always feel like you have a choice, and we may not always like the choices in front of us, especially when times are really tough, but you are always at choice in everything that you do or decide not to do.

MODIFIED FROM *SEVEN HABITS OF HIGHLY EFFECTIVE PEOPLE*
BY STEPHEN COVEY

When you feel that you don't have a choice, you may be dealing with feelings of hopelessness or a loss of control, or you are allowing fear to make decisions for you. Even in situations where you may not see other options, you always have a choice in how you respond, which really is the only thing in life that we have full control over.

When you feel that you don't have a choice, it's important to take a step back, out of your emotions, and think about what is really underway. Give yourself a fresh perspective to analyze the situation and decide how best you want to show up.

You Always Have Choice

Let me give you a personal example: what I call the "flood of 2019". At that time, I was living in Chicago in a four-unit condo building. As most people know, Chicago is known for its severe winters, wind, and cold, and I made it my personal mission to avoid the depths of a Chicago winter as often as I could by traveling to warmer locales.

That winter, while I was away, Chicago was hit with a polar vortex (i.e., very, very, very cold temperatures), and unfortunately, my upstairs neighbor's pipes froze and burst, flooding my condo as well as the unit beneath mine. Over three-quarters of my apartment had to be demolished, right down to the studs, and I was literally forced from my home for almost a year. During that time, (and even longer, almost two years), I fought with four different insurance companies to be able to rebuild and have it paid for.

Keep calm and control the controllables
— Unknown

When all of this was happening, I struggled with feelings of despair, anger, fear of losing my hard-earned savings, anxiety over when and how I would actually be able to move home again, and so much more.

After several months of navigating these emotions, I found myself in a place of depression, experiencing sleepless nights and even physical pain. I saw no hope and felt that I had no choice. I felt like a victim, as if this had all happened *to* me.

But even though I had no choice about being forced from my home, the reality of the situation was that I had choice over how much I let difficult things control my thoughts, feelings, and actions. My choice was either to remain stuck in a place of negativity and pain or to grieve the loss of my sanctuary and embrace my new normal.

Through tears and many anger-filled runs along Lakeshore Drive, the decision became clear. I chose to give myself time and space to grieve and then to move forward. While not a simple exercise by any means, recognizing I had a choice in how I allowed this difficult situation to impact me gave me the opportunity to take some of my power back, shift my energy into taking care of myself, and find joy and happiness in my life again.

Here are some other experiences that I've personally had that you might relate to:

- The time my boss took credit for my work. I had a choice to stay in the role or find a new job.
- When I was betrayed by a friend whom I fully trusted, I had a choice to confront them or put up a wall.
- When my apartment was burglarized, I had a choice to be afraid or find comfort in knowing my neighbors were watching and called the police.
- When I received surprising, negative feedback on a review, I had the choice to disregard the feedback or to work to shift perceptions.
- And so many others.

When you feel out of control and without choice, ask yourself the following questions to get back on track and remind yourself that you do actually have a choice:

1.   What are all the possible reasons why this is happening?

2. What possibilities are there in how I can navigate this situation?

3. How much do I want this situation to impact my overall energy, motivation, and life?

4. What is my desired reaction or response? Why?

5. What are some immediate steps that I *could* take in this situation?

By digging deeper, you'll find that you have choice in everything. And even though you may not always like the situation, you have the gift of being able to take full responsibility and accountability for yourself. And what greater choice is there than that?

That choice is often about deciding what you really want to focus on, what action (or inaction) you want to take, and/or how you want to feel before, during, and after this experience or challenge.

Choice is Another Word for Vision

When making the choice in how you show up, where you focus, and how you feel, you are ultimately setting your intention and creating a vision for who you want to be. That vision guides how you set your sights forward. It allows you to manage your energy and focus, and more importantly, it allows you to create goals and a plan to achieve them.

When we have a vision, we are aiming ourselves in a particular direction. This impacts our thoughts, feelings, and actions (or inactions). It allows us to see more, not less. After all, what we look for is what we will see. Here's an example: think about the last time you bought a new car. You chose that car because you liked the model, color, or price point, etc. And the moment that you drove that car off the lot or out of the driveway, you suddenly see that car everywhere. This is because you've now opened your mind to seeing this particular car, whereas you weren't looking for it before. The same holds true in where we choose to focus ourselves and our vision—we see what we want to see.

When you have a vision (and/or make a choice), you are taking the first step toward a successful result. You probably recognize these steps as the fundamentals of goal setting:

- Create a vision or a goal
- Put together a step-by-step action plan
- Take the first small step toward the vision or goal (and the second…and the third…)
- Ultimately achieve the vision / accomplish the goal
- Celebrate your success

By applying your choice (or vision), you will establish yourself as a powerful leader in your organization, within your network, within your family, and in your social circles. When you know what kind of leader you want to be, you will intentionally choose to become that leader. Without that vision and idea of what legacy you want to leave behind, you will certainly grow, but may achieve only a portion of what you could accomplish with vision and focus.

You have the choice—and the power—to be the most authentic and the best version of yourself, not force yourself into a cookie-cutter or commonly accepted standard of leadership. This is where all your awareness and choice come together to empower you to reDEFYne leadership.

CHAPTER 6

CRAFTING YOUR LEADERSHIP REDEFYNED™ STATEMENT AND LEADERSHIP VISION

N ow it's time to put pen to paper (or letters on the screen, depending on your preferred methodology) to help you determine your unique and authentic approach to Leadership reDEFYned™ to achieve the greatest success for yourself. Know that this is a process, so please dedicate time for reflection and processing information. Let go of any pressure to have the "right" answers immediately; the more time you spend on this, the more your vision will become clear.

> *If you don't know where you are going,*
> *you might wind up someplace else.*
> *— Yogi Berra*

We're going to walk through a six-step process together. We will also revisit this later in the book, so consider this section your warmup to get the juices flowing and give you space to truly understand what kind of leader you are today, and what you want to be in the future.

Now, grab your favorite notebook, pen, pencil, tablet, laptop, keyboard, or even voice recorder so you can begin drafting your roadmap to leadership reDEFYned™. Keep an eye out for the labels **Take Note** and **Pause for Reflection** to guide your work.

Step 1: What Kind of Leader Are You, Today?

First things first, you need to identify what makes you special and unique, as outlined in Chapter 4. This will help you land on your competitive advantage, your unique value proposition, mix of gifts, strengths, and talents, etc., that you and only you alone possess.

Be forewarned that this part will be hard. I find that most people struggle with this reflection and assessment because it requires a deep look within, and it requires self-promotion, which can feel like bragging and make people (I especially find this to be true for women) very uncomfortable.

But trust the process. This step is necessary so you can embrace what you already have working for you and know where you are starting from for future growth. Knowledge is power! Remember:

Awareness + Choice = *Intentional* Leadership

Take stock of where you are today. You may be able to do this on your own, but you are not alone if you want to tap into your community to get a solid read on what is and isn't working for you as a leader today.

Take Note: Make an inventory of your gifts, strengths, talents, and skills

Think about these from a professional perspective, but don't forget about your personal side, too. After all, we are looking for what makes you *you*, and that includes your interests and personality traits. Leadership reDEFYned™ is about authenticity; there should not be a significant difference between the work version of you and the outside-of-work version of you, it's all about intentionally choosing how you show up (remember the dials from Chapter 4).

As I mentioned earlier, if you get stuck, seek inspiration from those who know you well, such as your bosses, mentors, peers, friends, family, and significant others. Don't be afraid to reach out to prior employers or colleagues, too. Everyone will have an opinion about you, and by simply asking, "What do you think are my top three gifts (or skills or talents)?" you'll get some great answers. Some may be very consistent, which will offer validation of how you are showing up today, and others may be outliers based on the relationship or situation.

You can also get inspiration from past performance reviews or a "save me for a bad day" file of compliments and accolades, from awards or recognitions you've received over the years, or by creating a love/neutral/hate list about the work you do. (Note: if you don't have a "save me for a bad day" file, I strongly encourage you to start this. It is a folder where you save thanks, kudos, recognition for a job well done, your exemplary leadership skills, etc. These pieces of information or inputs can be powerful when you need a pick-me-up, or to write your annual self-assessment, etc., and certainly come in handy when creating (or revisiting) your leadership reDEFYned™ vision.)

As you start this part of the exercise, make this an all-encompassing inventory, and try to respond without judgment. All you are doing at this stage is collecting information. As much as you can, step away from judgment, imposter syndrome, or discomfort that you have in writing these things down.

Pause for Reflection

Answer the following questions as honestly as you can:

- What talents and gifts do I have, or what do people often compliment me for?
- What skills, experience, and/or training do I have? Be sure to think about both hard and soft skills.
- What am I really good at doing, or what do I get praised for on my performance reviews?
- I feel I add the most value to others in doing _____. Or, what gets me the most excited to do?

Step 2: What Kind of Leader Do You Want to Be?

Many people have an easier time with Step 2 than Step 1 because it is outside of ourselves. This is where you consider what "good" could look like for you, what qualities and traits you admire in others, and/or what skills or experiences you might want to master as you think about your leadership impact or legacy.

Let's be clear—this is not goal-setting. We aren't there yet. This step is about exploring the possibilities and understanding what you are attracted to. It's about exploring where you *could* go, not necessarily where you have to or will go.

Take Note: Capture your potential leadership aspirations

To complete this portion of the exercise, consider the following questions:

- What leaders do I look up to, and what qualities or skills do I admire about them? (These can be people you know, historical figures, influential figures in the media, or even fictional characters, like my personal admiration of Wendy Rhoades in the show *Billions*. Who have you witnessed in a leadership position and thought, that's a really great leader because...)

- What do they do (or have) that I find meaningful and important?
- When I think of great leadership, I think of these qualities or skills: _____.
- When I reflect on the best leaders I've worked with, they did _____ and didn't _____. (The inverse of this also works: when I reflect on the worst leaders I've worked with, they did _____ and didn't _____.)

When the vision is clear, strategy is easy
— Unknown

Your vision of great leadership is *your vision*—not the vision of society or traditional leadership standards. Consider the Law of Attraction, which proposes that *what you put out is what you get back*. In this exercise, we are flipping it around: what you want to get back is what you are attracted to, and therefore what you want to put out there.

Similar to Step 1, make this an all-encompassing list and don't overthink what you include. Again, this is about collecting inventory of possibilities and isn't locking into any one thing or another, yet. So don't let any limiting beliefs about your abilities or fears of your aspirations get in the way of compiling this list.

Pause for Reflection

Spend time in deep reflection to analyze and understand what you believe great leadership is and what your future leadership could look like. Don't let other people define this aspiration for you.

Step 3: Where Do You Want to Focus?

At this point, you should have two very healthy lists: one for who you are today and another for where you might want to go. Now, let's prioritize what matters most to you.

This may feel easier said than done. It's easy to get in your head and overthink things, to look at the lists through others' eyes or assumed expectations, to diminish your belief in your ability to succeed, to make excuses (e.g., I don't have time or money to grow in that way), or to feel insecure about naming your gifts and aspirations. And the list of excuses and negative self-talk can go on and on.

We don't want to give any power to those excuses or inner fears, so eliminate those voices or concerns right now and focus on what your body tells you. In her article "How to Stop Overthinking and Start Trusting Your Gut," for the *Harvard Business Review*, Melodie Wilding explained how scientists call the stomach a second brain. It turns out that "following your gut" is more than just a clever saying! Your body is your largest sensor and the easiest way to know when you're on track or not. By paying attention to the signals your body gives (a.k.a., awareness), the more aligned you are to your authentic step into Leadership reDEFYned™.

Take Note: Analyze and prioritize your leadership attributes

For Step 3 of this exploration, look at both lists and read each attribute out loud. As you read each one, check how your body reacts, including your gut, your heart, your mind, and your breath. Notice when your body sends signals of excitement, like stomach flips, warmth, faster breathing, or a flushed face, and when it sends signals of misalignment, like stomach pain, chest pressure, tightness in your throat, or discomfort.

Consider when you feel positive, neutral, or disenchanted with a concept. As you sense or feel the positive concepts, circle them. Any negative or neutral concepts, scratch them out.

Review the circled items and prioritize them, cutting the list down to a number that feels reasonable to you. This may be six attributes, or it may be eight; there is no rule about how many qualities and aspirations you need to have or will focus on. Keep in mind that the more you have on the list, the more complex it is, so I often recommend focusing on five at any given time.

Know that as you grow as a leader, so will your focus and opportunity, so this is not a set-in-stone be-all-end-all exercise. Revisit it and update it regularly—I recommend at least annually or when you conduct goal-setting.

Now, look at the combined and prioritized list again to make sure that you've narrowed it down to the most relevant, most important to you today and for your future. Create a new, clean, final list of the leadership attributes that you want to prioritize now and will become your leadership vision moving forward.

When you have narrowed down the list to the current and aspirational qualities that feel comprehensive to you, both current and aspirational qualities, move on to step 4.

If you get stuck, consider resetting your energy by taking a break, doing some stretches, doing breathing exercises, turning on some creative music, or doing whatever you need to do to reset your energy and your perspective.

Ready?

How to Reset Your Energy

- Change your scenery to reset your mind
- Stretch or exercise to get endorphins flowing
- Superhero pose to increase confidence
- Play music to tap into more parts of your brain
- Read it out loud (and see how it feels for you)
- Meditate solo or listen to a guided meditation
- Do a centering exercise
- Close your eyes and envision yourself succeeding
- Take a deep breath in focusing on positivity; exhale letting go of any negativity (and repeat)
- Walk away and come back with fresh eyes

Pause for Reflection

Close your eyes and imagine that you are retiring from your very successful career at whatever age you would like to retire. You've been able to achieve all of your professional and personal goals and have mastered this list of leadership attributes (from Step 3) that you've identified thus far. Beyond that, you've seen great successes, and you've positively impacted the world around you. You have created a strong leadership legacy, and you are extremely proud of the leader you've become.

Step 4: What is Your Leadership Legacy (Your Why)?

In this step, you'll use your final list of prioritized leadership attributes to develop your leadership vision. This will be your Leadership reDEFYned™ Statement.

Keep your eyes closed and really envision what this looks like, what this feels like, and what this sounds like. Remove any barriers, rationale, or obstacles that might come up, and just dream for a few minutes. Imagine that you have all the skills and resources available to you to get exactly where you want to go.

Take Note: Write down the leadership dreams you envision for yourself to connect to your why

Now, write it all down. Reflect on that emotion and what your impact could be. Ask yourself what that world would be like. Write down specifics, including what your leadership looks like, how it feels, how others receive you, what type of work you are doing, how you are making a difference in the world, what results you are striving for, and what you are really good at. By connecting to this future state, you can connect more deeply to your inner authenticity and your *why*. This connection will not only enable you to step into your greatest leadership abilities, but it will ensure that your growth is meaningful and will unleash your fullest potential.

Again, if you get stuck, do something to spark creativity, shift your perspective, and give you energy. Move your body, ignite your senses, and start fresh.

When you have this future legacy in your mind and loosely noted, it's time to craft your Leadership reDEFYned™ Statement. This vision should be a simple mantra that has meaning and influence to you. It can be a sentence or two, or it can be a few key words that empower you and remind you of your goals and your focus.

The words don't need to be perfect, and they don't need to make sense to anyone but you. They will serve as inspiration, direction, alignment, and understanding of self, and they serve as your guiding light to navigate how you lead and how you successfully reDEFYne leadership.

Take Note: Draft your Leadership reDEFYned™ statement

If you get stuck, here is a template you can consider:

I am a _____ leader

that _____

because I _____

to deliver _____

Example: I am a <u>passionate and inspirational</u> leader that <u>focuses on helping others become the best version of themselves that they possibly</u> can be because <u>I believe we are all leaders and know that in doing so, I help</u> to deliver <u>powerhouse leaders and greater positive impact to the world</u>.

I encourage you to not only craft this statement, but to read it out loud and ask your body to validate that this vision or statement is aligned with you to your core. I encourage you to share it with individuals you trust as well to help ensure that you're tapping into your authenticity for today and for tomorrow.

Step 5: Put It All Together

Now that you have the vision and an understanding of ways you can achieve great success (aka your why), let's put it all together and create not only a goal for your leadership but an action plan to ensure that you are successful in stepping fully into this vision of the great leader that you can be:

1. Look at your Leadership reDEFYned™ Statement and reflect on how much you are already living it today, on a scale of 1 to 10 with one being not at all, and ten being all day without question.

2. Based on that rating, consider what you can start, stop, or change to get closer to a desired future rating (closer to that 10) and make a note of these possibilities. (Note: If you gave yourself a 10 already, consider what stretch opportunities and aspirations you might want to further explore from Steps 2 and 3.)

3. Assess what the missing pieces are, or any gaps or opportunities, and create an overarching goal (or set of goals if needed) for what you'd like to achieve as a leader in the next year or timeframe of your liking. Consider the SMART goal structure as you craft this: specific, measurable, actionable, relevant, and time-based.

4. Break down that goal into smaller SMART steps so you can begin to take action. (See Chapter 13 for more detail about Steps 4 through 6).

5. Consider enlisting an accountability partner and setting timelines (there's that time-based part again...) to keep progressing toward your leadership vision goal.

6. Achieve that goal, and celebrate! Celebrate not only the goal achievement, but all of the small wins along the way,

too! This can be as simple as acknowledging your progress to yourself or sharing the win with someone and taking a moment to acknowledge the accomplishment.

Think about what will make you feel proud of your accomplishment and remember the effort you put forth to get there. This step is crucial in crushing your milestones to achieve the larger goal. Is it treating yourself to a nice dinner, a glass of wine, or an unexpected present? Perhaps it's sending a celebratory email to your team or having a small gathering with friends.

I personally love sharing the win with a close friend and having that moment of celebration together When I verbally state it, it makes the win real, and I also get recognition for the win, giving myself a moment of joy.

Take Note: You can use this template to gather your thoughts or document them in another way that makes sense to you. However you do it, the key is to write it down so you can reference it, remember it, revisit it, and reflect on all the things you've accomplished in your leadership journey.

1A. Your Leadership redEFYned™ Statement:	
1B. Today's Rating (Scale of 1 – 10, with 1 being not at all and 10 being all day, every day)	**2A. Desired Future Rating** (Scale of 1 – 10, with 1 being not at all and 10 being all day, every day)
2B. What does good look like? (i.e., what does this leadership vision look like when you've achieved it?)	
3. What is missing today that will help you become the leader you want to be in the future?	
4. SMART Goal:	
Step 1:	
Step 2:	
Step 3 (etc.):	
5) Accountability Partner	**6) Celebration Plan**

Now it's time to put those goals and action plans into motion! Note: We will dig deeper into this in Chapter 13, so it is perfectly acceptable to have a higher-level plan here. As you learn more about Leadership reDEFYned™ and the 3 Principles, you may want to enhance your goal(s) and/or action plans too.

Step 6: Rinse and Repeat

As you continue to grow and develop as a leader, reflect on your Leadership reDEFYned™ Statement and assess it periodically. Understand how you're growing and achieving that vision, and take time to reflect on whether it needs to evolve along with you. Ask yourself how your actions and decisions align with your authentic self and where else you can focus or grow to become the most successful leader that you can be.

By repeating these steps, you will have the ability to not only see how you've grown but also how you mature as a leader over time. I highly recommend repeating these steps every few years as you grow and evolve your leadership skills; I especially recommend revisiting Step 5 on an annual basis to ensure that all the decisions you are making, all the communications you put out, and how you support those around you demonstrate your Leadership reDEFYned™ Statement and vision for the legacy that you want to leave behind.

CHAPTER 7

WHAT (REALLY) IS GREAT LEADERSHIP?

As you've learned thus far, Leadership reDEFYned™ is based on the premise that we can no longer hold everyone to the same leadership standards and that authentic and intentional leadership will result in greater outcomes for the individual leader, the people they encounter, and their organization as a whole. Knowing and honoring who you are, understanding who you want to be, and creating a vision for the future will set you up for great leadership success and significant positive impact.

At this point in the book, we've walked our way through intentional leadership, which is essential to your leadership and core to the leadership reDEFYned™ model. This focus will set you up to be a good leader.

Awareness + Choice = *Intentional* Leadership

You also have reflected on intentional leadership as you developed your Leadership reDEFYned™ Statement. That statement is your roadmap for how you'd like to grow as a leader and how you can put intentional leadership into action.

LEADERSHIP
REDEFYNED

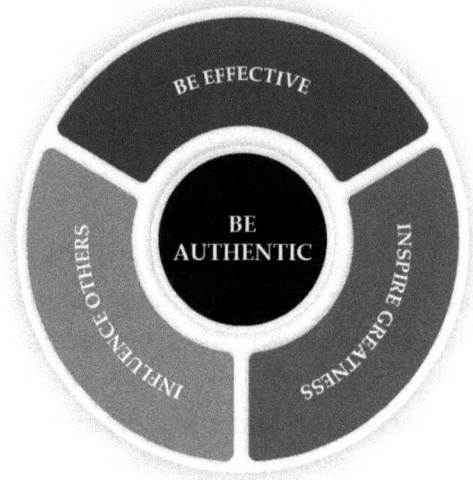

We also started to explore the three principles of leadership:

- Principle 1: Be Effective
- Principle 2: Influence Others
- Principle 3: Inspire Greatness

The combination of putting these principles into action along with your Leadership reDEFYned™ Statement will take you from good to great, making you the powerhouse leader that is already inside you, waiting to be fully realized.

So, let's make this clear: the equation for great leadership is:

Intentional Leadership x 3 Principles of Leadership
= *Great Leadership*

The inclusion of these 3 principles will exponentially increase your leadership abilities and create a positive impact for your team, your organization, your family, and yourself. With this, you will inspire others to become great leaders, following your example of being authentic and not having to fit into that overly common and minimally diverse leadership box that prohibits us from being as successful as we can be.

When you embrace these collectively and with your authenticity, you will step into a leadership approach that is more powerful, more meaningful, and just *more* than you likely ever imagined possible.

CHAPTER 8

LEADERSHIP REDEFYNED™
PRINCIPLE 1: BE EFFECTIVE

T he very first principle and most foundational area of great leadership is efficacy, or being effective in your role.

---

ef·fi·ca·cy
/'efəkəsē/
noun

The ability to produce a desired or intended result

Efficacy or being effective in your role is simply doing what you say you are going to do. Efficacy is demonstrating the behavior that you want your team to follow. Efficacy sets the stage for your team to value you and trust that you'll actually be there for them, that you'll deliver for them, and that you'll be a support, not a hindrance, to the success of the project or initiative at hand.

Efficacy is also making sure that you are removing any roadblocks or challenges that your team has so they can be effective in their roles.

But before we get too far into efficacy for others, let's first focus on what it means for ourselves. It means that we are productive with the right mindset, setting an example for those around us. At a granular level, being effective also means that we are organized, have prioritized our workload, and are timely with our delivery.

Organization	Prioritization	Time Management
Knowing what is what (i.e organization of stuff)	Knowing what you want to do with it (i.e organization of your focus)	Actually doing it (i.e organization of your time)

To Be Effective, We Must Be Productive

Productivity, scientifically speaking, is the measure of input and the rate of output, or basically, how much work is produced by a certain amount of resources. Productivity can often be measured by output (e.g., how much did you get done), by speed (e.g., how fast did you get something done), or a combination of both. Simply put, productivity is doing more with less, capitalizing on the ability to be effective in all that you do. Productivity is also a feeling or inner acknowledgement of focus, clarity, and alignment.

While we often focus on the external components of productivity, such as the efficient and effective use of resources like time, equipment, and people (including ourselves), I argue that to be truly productive, we must also focus on and pay attention to the *internal components*. When you are internally aligned to what you are doing, you will have more buy-in and a stronger connection to your "why" (your real motivation). That inner motivation is directly connected to the energy that you bring to getting "it" done.

Productivity is loosely half action (what you do) and half mindset (your source of motivation).

Productivity is not about doing work for the sake of doing work. It's about doing the most valuable work for the sake of the goal, yourself, your team, or your organization.

Productivity is also about knowing when and how you work best. For example, I am not a morning person. For me, it is virtually impossible to step into work first thing in the morning and develop deep strategy or creative content. I'm more mentally capable between 10 am and 12 pm, or 3 to 5 pm. In the other hours of the workday, I know that administrative tasks can be achieved without that mental load. I know how my body functions, and I plan my work around those insights so that I am able to be productive throughout the entire day with different types of work based on my energy and mental state.

Other fun facts about productivity:

- Scientists believe that people are generally more productive throughout the workday if they start their morning by **working out.**
- **Tuesday** is believed to be the most productive day of the standard work week.
- Generally, people are the most productive between **8–9 am** and **4–5 pm.**
- Adults who get 7.5–9 hours of sleep/night can be up to **20% more productive** daily.
- After working 40 hours a week, productivity **decreases by 50%.**

While these are generalizations, the most important thing you can take away from this section is that you possess a unique approach to productivity. You must understand what times of day are better for you mentally, whether a morning or an afternoon workout will benefit you, whether you can maintain your ability to be effective after 40 hours, etc. The more you understand these things, the easier it will be for you to be a highly effective and productive leader.

To Be Productive, We Must Choose the Right Mindset

Our mindset and related energy are critical for productivity and effectiveness. To bring that to light, I like to reference a framework from *The Institute for Professional Excellence in Coaching* called The Range of Engagement©. In the Range of Engagement framework, you can assess you or your team's engagement in a particular job or relationship, which ultimately connects to both the effectiveness of the task at hand as well as the results of the task as it's completed.

To understand the Range of Engagement, let's move from the left side to the right side of the diagram. As you shift between the phases, your energy, mindset, and level of engagement (aka effectiveness) increases, and therefore the likelihood for success also increases.

Range of Engagement

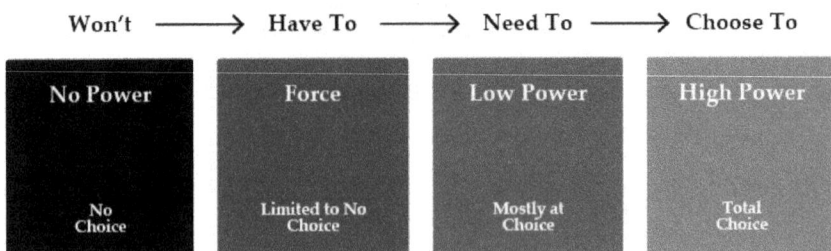

| Won't | ⟶ | Have To | ⟶ | Need To | ⟶ | Choose To |

No Power	Force	Low Power	High Power
No Choice	Limited to No Choice	Mostly at Choice	Total Choice

Provided by The Institute for
Professional Excellence in Coaching

- **Won't:** At the far left, you have a "won't" perspective or attitude. This is very much a victim mentality and a direct connection to feeling powerless and without choice. It's the idea that life is happening to you and there is nothing you can do about it, and so you *don't* do anything about it. This is the least effective mindset, as it limits your potential and opportunity for action. **Example:** *I won't go to the gym (because you are telling me to).*

- **Have to:** The next phase of engagement is "have to." This mindset tends to be a short-term outlook and is directly connected to fear. "I have to complete the task in front of me or else…" Often, when you are in the "have to" mindset, you will exert more energy fighting through the obstacles or challenges in front of you. You will try to take control of as much as you can to manage the feeling of having minimal choice in what you do. It is overcompensation and stems from a desire to control everything when previously you felt that you had control over nothing. Although you're taking action, it's much more difficult to be effective because you're exerting excess energy to power through the situation, which is not sustainable and ultimately will get in the way of your greater success. **Example:** *I have to go to the gym (or else I will gain weight).*

- **Need to:** The third phase is "need to", where you feel you have more power and choice. You look for opportunities in the tasks at hand rather than taking no action or fighting your way through them. Thus, you will have higher levels of engagement and effectiveness and feel more optimistic, with a greater sense of connection to the community around you. However, because this phase is still tied to "if I do this, then X will happen," there are still elements of consequence. So, while this phase offers a more optimistic outlook with greater focus and intent, there is not always a full connection between those actions and your own buy-in. **Example:** *I need to go to the gym (to take better care of myself).*

- **Chose to:** Finally, to the far right is the most powerful mindset of "choose to," where you have the most buy-in and connection to your why and, therefore, will be the most effective version of yourself. In this phase, you have complete choice in what you do, resulting in more feelings of control, energy, and enthusiasm. The direct connection between who you are and what you do in this phase makes it more enjoyable. **Example:** *I choose to go to the gym (and will have higher energy, a better workout, and long-term success).*

When you lead from a "choose to" mindset, you become more effective. You believe in your gifts and skills as a leader and view your role as creating opportunities for growth and development on both business and personal levels. You choose to experience your role as a leader. You recognize that your efforts may or may not turn out as expected, so you lead with a curiosity about what lies around the corner. "Choose to" leaders create productivity even in the worst conditions.

Consider this: When you are an engaged leader, choosing to be effective, you will have more success, guaranteed. The less engaged you are, the less aware you are of your choices and your ability to create, and the less likely you are to achieve success or even feel successful. Note: That doesn't mean it will always be easy and there won't be bumps in the road, but you will have the mindset, energy, and effectiveness to keep moving forward.

Your level of engagement also affects your ability to influence and inspire others. (Spoiler alert: That's how the three principles of leadership build upon each other.) The more aware of who you are as a leader, the more successful you will be in leading yourself (first) and others (second) to success.

Pause for Reflection

How would you rate your productivity on a regular basis?

What time of day or day of the week works best for you to have "think" time versus "do" time?

When do you have a "choose to" mindset vs a "need to", "have to" or "won't" mindset?

What parts of your role add to your energy versus deplete your energy?

How can you enhance your ability to be productive with a great mindset?

To Be Effective, We Must Be Organized, Prioritized, and Timely

To be an effective leader, organization, prioritization, and time management must go hand in hand and feed into our ability to be productive. These three words are often used interchangeably and are certainly interconnected, but each has its own merits for discussion.

There are thousands upon thousands of books and resources available on organization, prioritization, and time management, so I won't turn this into an all-encompassing "how to" but rather will share some highlights that will add to your ability to be an effective leader.

Organization

Organization is the mother of all time savers—your most precious and non-renewable resource. When your documents, emails, and project lists are organized, you save time in knowing what to do and where to find what you need, making it easier to move between tasks and meet your deadlines and commitments. It also reduces your stress because it frees your mind to focus on the aspects of the work rather than the extraneous steps of finding, worrying, and forgetting.

In addition, when you have lower stress and more time, you can be more creative with less lift. When the pressure is on and the stress is high, your body will naturally go into fix-it mode, which drastically reduces your ability to approach to the situation with creativity and innovation. It puts you in *do* mode rather than *think* mode, where you can contemplate all the possibilities for the best possible results.

To be organized, consider the following:

- **Create a master list.** Write down (or type) everything that is needed so you see it in one place and can start to make sense of it.
- **Give everything a home**. This may be a folder on your computer or a desk drawer designed to save time and energy finding things. It also offers peace of mind in your subconscious because you know that everything has a place.
- **Remove the junk or clutter from your workspace and life.** This helps to free your mind and open up that creative side of yourself.
- **Declutter, file, and update every day**. Organization is not a one-and-done thing. It's a daily effort. Consider if this is a great activity to start or end your day with.

- **Consider other organizational tools.** Project management software, team-sharing programs, reminders and task lists, and automations can help make this an easier lift.
- **Start small with changes.** Grandiose efforts take time, and they usually don't stick, so implement small organizational changes one at a time so the habits stick.
- **Revisit what is working and what isn't regularly**. At the end of every day, week, month, or quarter assess your efforts so you can continually optimize your approach.

Prioritization

Prioritization is the art of knowing (and doing) what's most important, what adds the most value, and what makes the greatest impact. It is a clear-cut way of determining what to focus on and in what order. More importantly, it helps you identify what *not* to focus on. It enables you to align tasks and initiatives to your own personal values and value you can contribute to others, resulting in authenticity, greater satisfaction and joy, and increased energy and output (productivity).

There are many great tools for prioritization, but my favorite of all time (and still the most salient in my opinion), is from Stephen Covey's *The 7 Habits of Highly Effective People*. This simple prioritization tool is based on the Eisenhower Matrix and asks two powerful questions: Is this important or not? Is this urgent or not?

By answering those two questions about each task, you can determine what to do with it.

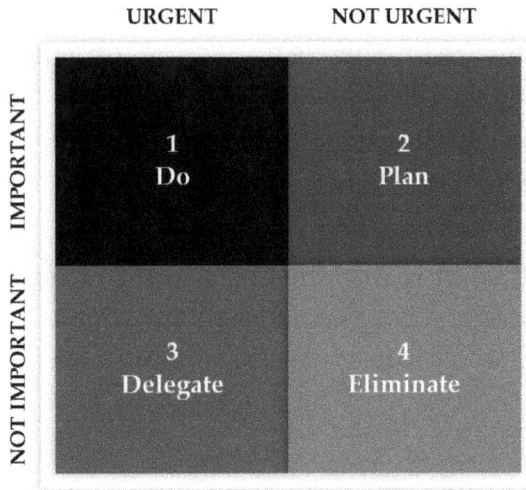

The Eisenhower Matrix

As busy leaders, most people focus on quadrant 1: urgent *and* important. While effective, this can result in more stress, burnout, and fatigue, and will eventually lead to greater health and wellness issues. The ideal place for you to be as a leader is in quadrant 2: important but not urgent. This zone is great for strategic planning, thoughtfulness and intention, team and personal development, and more. It is essentially focusing on the good stuff and giving yourself time to do it.

Typically, as leaders grow up, they get stuck in quadrants 3 and 4. Those areas *feel* important, but they aren't really. We see this most when people move from individual contributors to managers without the proper training and guidance. These leaders tend to focus on what they know they can do, so they stay in the weeds. They get sucked into too many details and lose focus on what is the most valuable (and important) use of their time.

When prioritizing, quadrant 3 is an area where you can focus on growing your team (and yourself) by delegating and giving more opportunities for others to learn in a lower-risk environment. By embracing a fast-failure mindset and releasing control of doing, leaders can then focus on the value-adds that most align with their skills and values.

Finally, quadrant 4, if we're being totally honest, is full of time sucks and energy drains and for the most part should really be avoided. Why take on a task if it is not important and not urgent? Does it really need to happen at all?

When teaching my clients about prioritization, I encourage them to take this grid and plot their day, while also managing requests that come in at the moment. This will help to build the muscle memory to be able to more quickly decide what is the best thing for you to do.

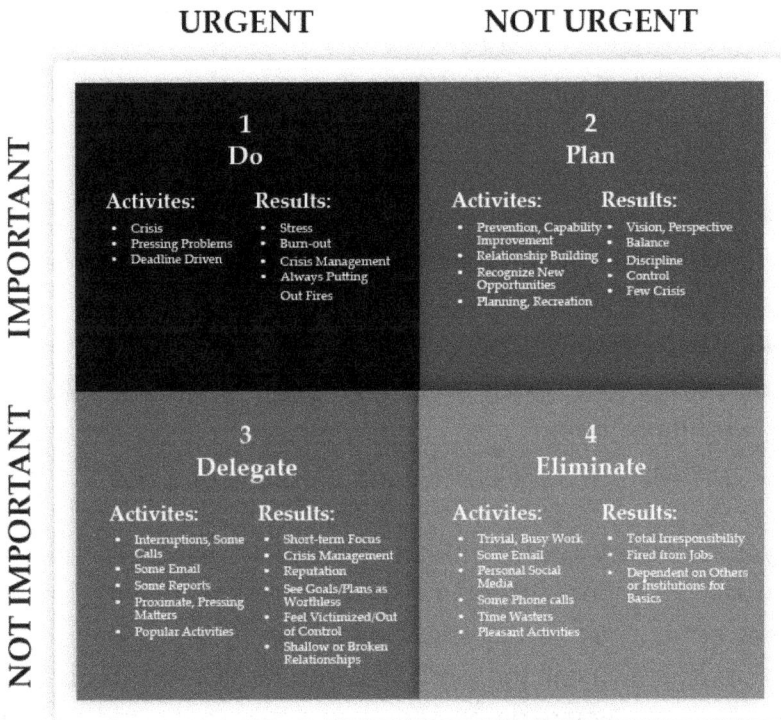

The Eisenhower Matrix

As you work on prioritization, consider these additional tips to decide what to do now and what to do later or not at all:

- Know your values and the value you can offer to others. If you don't know these things or don't feel confident in how you answer this, consider taking a values assessment or revisit your answers from Chapter 4 to understand your value.

- Ask yourself if it is urgent or important to assess whether it's worth your time and energy.

- Ask yourself if it ladders up to the organization's goals, your team's goals, or your own personal goals.

- Write your to-do list and find ways to indicate priority, whether it's the quadrants, in order of importance, with color coding, deadlines, or another unique system that works for you.

- Know your "why" and connect the tasks to it. If they don't align, ask if it's really needed or necessary for you personally to do it, or can be delegated out).

- When given a task or a request, create a plan for how and when to get it done, especially for larger tasks with multiple steps.

- Be willing to reevaluate your priorities regularly.

As you consider where and how you focus yourself and your priorities, I encourage you to further explore delegation and empowerment as principles. Delegation doesn't mean that you're giving away all the work that you don't want to do, but it does mean that you're empowering your team or partners to own part of the process, grow and develop their skills, and enable true value to be added to the organization. A few other rules I like to reference when it comes to delegation:

- Keep the project when it must be done a specific way, but delegate if there is more than one right way.
- Keep the project when it takes longer to explain than to complete, but delegate if it's a skill the employee needs to learn.
- Keep the project when you really enjoy it, but delegate if it's no longer in your job description or will hold someone else back.

Time Management

Finally, we have time management. Let's think about this as the glue that holds organization and prioritization together. After all, if you can find it and you think it's important, you need to carve out the time to do it.

When it comes to time management, consider what we spoke about earlier and ask yourself: What time of day am I at my best to do this? In other words, when are you the most energetic, strategic, or focused? And alternatively, when are you the most lethargic and distracted?

If you don't already know this, pay attention to how you are feeling and your motivation over the next week or so. Observe your body, your energy, and your mindset to better understand what time of day is best for you to work on strategic thinking projects versus answering emails, versus reading or professional development activities. As you learn when you work best, your time management skills will drastically improve.

I also encourage you to keep a log of how you spend your time for a week to see where you might have some quadrant 4 opportunities to say no to.

I have always lived my life by making lists: lists of people to call, lists of ideas, lists of companies to set up, lists of people who can make things happen. Each day I work through these lists and that sequence of calls propels me forward.
— Richard Branson

Here are a few more time management tips for your consideration:

- **List your to-dos.** This is a thread that ties organization, prioritization, and time management together. Lists do not have to be a forever thing, but are extremely helpful when creating new habits for your focus.

- **Give yourself deadlines.** And if they are big ones, break them down into a project plan with steps and interim deadlines.

- **Seek accountability.** If setting a deadline for yourself isn't effective (because let's be honest, we tend to prioritize other people's needs over our own), tell someone your deadline and ask for support with accountability.

- **Use your calendar to manage your time.** Yes, that's an obvious statement, but in addition to adding appointments and meetings, block out time for important tasks, especially those that require thinking and reduced distractions.

- **Minimize distractions.** When you are in that time block, turn everything else off or hide it. Turn off notifications on your phone, email, and social media. Put your phone where you can't easily reach it. Close your door. Do whatever you need to do to stay focused.

- **Know your work style**. If being in the office helps you focus when you have bigger initiatives, great. If being home is better for you, then do that. Whether you prefer listening to music or being in complete silence, honor that. This is another aspect of being authentic: know yourself and take advantage of what works for you rather than trying to fit into a box.

- **Reset to enable focus.** Consider meditation, breathing exercises, and physical activity to reset your mind when needed. If you're struggling with a task, go outside for a walk or do a 5-minute meditation.

- **Understand and set boundaries.** Identify what boundaries you need to set in order to be successful. Define them, share them, and honor them. It is OK to say no to requests, or to say yes, but not right now.

- **Delegate non-urgent tasks.** Focus your time and energy on the things that need to be done specifically by you and hand off anything that someone else can take on.

- **Know when "good" is good enough**. Strive for progress over perfection and know when it is time to close out a task or drop a goal, either temporarily or permanently.

- **Celebrate the wins.** Whether the accomplishments are big or small, recognize your accomplishments to keep you motivated and inspired.

I've found that over the years, I best manage my time and ability to be effective with my time in a few ways:

1. I start each morning by reviewing my commitments for the day and creating a list of my top priorities for the day. These are my must-dos before I can stop working that day. Sometimes this is a list written on a sheet of paper, sometimes I use Notes in my iPhone, and sometimes I use a dry-erase board. The format is less important for me than the fact that I write it down to make sure it happens that day.

2. I review my calendar to see where and how these priorities can fit into the day to ensure that this is a realistic and achievable plan for the day. I time block where I can or make decisions about potentially working through lunch or later that day, etc.

3. Email correspondence happens between these activities. Ashton Kutcher actually has a philosophy that when we respond to or prioritize emails, we are prioritizing what others need from us, not what we need to deliver. I have found that emails can be a big time suck for me so I manage them between activities vs making that my central focus, especially first thing in the morning.

As you continue to develop your leadership style and advance in your career, I encourage you to analyze what makes you more productive and effective, what tools or support services can you tap into to be more organized, prioritized, and timely. The answer is different for everyone, so finding what works best for you will set you up for long-term success and will also help demonstrate possibilities to your team and those around you.

Efficacy is the first principle in Leadership reDEFYned™ for a reason. You have to be effective and competent in your role if you expect to lead others and create the impact that you want to. To put it simply, efficacy is your ability to do what it is that you say you are going to do, when and how you say you are going to do it. It includes productivity, organization, prioritization, and time management.

Pause for Reflection

Please take a few moments to reflect on what being effective means to you.

- Are you doing what you say you will do today?
- How productive, organized, prioritized, or timely are you?
- What areas are you already thriving in?
- What areas may need some work?

Review your Leadership reDEFYned statement. Consider what you've learned about Principle 1: Efficacy that will need to be applied to bring your leadership vision to life.

CHAPTER 9

LEADERSHIP REDEFYNED™ PRINCIPLE 2: INFLUENCE OTHERS

Principle 2 of Leadership reDEFYned™ is the ability to influence those around you. If there is one thing I want you to learn about this principle, it is this: When you influence others to action instead of using power and authority to demand action, you will see greater results.

The key to successful leadership today
is influence, not authority.
— Ken Blanchard

Influence is the ability to create positive movement without using power or demanding change. Influence is moving individuals to be on the same page about a project or initiative. Influence is getting disparate ideas to align to a unified approach. Influence is a powerful leadership skill.

When it comes to the ability to influence, leaders often think about the people that directly report or answer to them, but being able to influence others is a great skill holistically, especially when you need to influence those who don't report or answer to you. This includes other team members, peers, leadership, family, and social circles. And because it has a broader reach, it's important to keep in mind that influence is not the same as authority.

Being able to influence others, especially without flexing your power, is an art form that boils down to social and self-awareness. (There's that reference to emotional intelligence again.) Once you can assess those together to determine your best path forward, you can be a powerful influencer in getting others to connect with and execute the message that you are sending or the vision you are creating.

Influence Is About Listening and Communicating

Most people would say influence is all about communication, but you cannot communicate effectively if you are not fully listening. Listening is the most important aspect of communication and often the first to be missed.

When you truly listen to what is said and what is not, you can better understand the world around you, and you continue to learn and grow, refining your leadership approach. Listening allows you to consider what others want and need, thus increasing your social awareness (one-half of emotional intelligence).

When you learn to truly listen, hear, see, and intuitively understand, you can be a powerful force as a leader and as a contributing member of positive change. Some of the many benefits of listening include gaining a greater understanding of the perspectives, concerns, ideas, and needs of the people around you. It also allows you to seek to understand first before jumping into action.

Learning to listen is also about listening to yourself. Remember, your body is the largest sensor of what is working and what isn't.

Your body sends you signals, and if you really pay attention, those signals will help you to be more self-aware and in line with your authentic self, setting you up for greater leadership success. Listening to yourself means paying attention to and understanding body signals and your thoughts, feelings, and actions (or inactions). It also means sifting out the negative self-talk and insecurity. The more you know this, the more awareness and opportunity you'll find to truly be there for others.

It is ironic that although listening is a critical element of effective communication, few people do it well. Research tells us that when we struggle to listen, we may be distracted by:

- Unclear words
- New and uncomfortable situations
- Preconceived notions
- Physical stress
- Our emotions
- Lack of trust or respect in those speaking (or any other limiting emotion)
- Our fears and insecurities

Most of the successful people I've known are the
ones who do more listening than talking.
— Bernard Baruch

But the most common reason we struggle to listen is that we are preparing our response or next question rather than being fully present.

How Do You Become a Great Listener?

First things first, consider the concept of the beginner's mind as your most basic and possibly most impactful approach to listening. The term beginner's mind comes from the Zen Buddhism concept *shoshin*, which means listen with an open mind, an eagerness to learn, and without judgment or preconceived notions. You should have no filters and be fully present in that moment, taking in the information (both verbal and nonverbal) as if it is the first time you've ever heard it. This approach to listening increases your energy and connection with those speaking to you. The speaker you are listening to can literally feel your intention and focus on them, opening them up to greater possibilities, too.

Here are a few ways you can become a great listener:

- **Be fully present.** This means avoiding distracted listening. Clear your mind of all thoughts and preconceived notions, and utilize an improv approach, meaning you can only react to what is being said versus planning out the next steps in the conversation.

- **No judgments or agendas.** Remove your bias and judgment from the conversation and check your motivation on what you want to say before you actually say it.

- **Reflect what is said.** By repeating or reiterating what the other person has said or is feeling, you demonstrate that you have heard and care about what they're saying.

- **Show that you are really listening.** Stemming from *active listening*, the term coined by Carl Rogers and Richard Farson in 1957, you want to physically show that you are paying attention. Use your body language to demonstrate that you are invested by leaning in, nodding your head, or raising your eyebrows. Verbal cues like "uh-huh's" or "yes's" also prove that you are engaged and listening.

Levels of Listening

There are ample resources available to improve your listening skills. For the sake of this simplicity, I'm going to focus on the three-level structure that both the Institute for Professional Excellence in Coaching (iPEC) and Co-active Coaching subscribe to.

Levels of Listening

Level	Purpose	Action	Focus	Simplified
1	To Speak	Internal	Subjective	Me
2	To Hear	Focused	Objective	You
3	To Understand	Global	Intuitive	Us

Provided by The Institute for
Professional Excellence in Coaching

Level 1: Subjective Listening

This type of listening is primarily focused on listening to yourself, your thoughts, your opinions, your worldview (your lens), or your biases. Often, this is when you are thinking about the next thing to say, your to-do list, or what your family members are doing at that very moment. It is distracted listening and means that you are not fully hearing the other person in the conversation. This type of listening is also common when people feel the need to be in control.

> **Example:** I'm really upset about the feedback we got from the client on this project.

Subjective response: Yeah, I worked really hard on it.

Level 2: Objective Listening

At this level, you are focused completely on the person who is speaking and have successfully eliminated judgment, bias, and distractions. You are not thinking about the past or the future, just the present moment and the words that are being spoken to you. While level 2 or objective listening is very effective, far more effective than level 1, the challenge is that you may miss the actual intent behind the words—the things that aren't being said but just implied.

> **Example:** I'm really upset about the feedback we got from the client on this project.
>
> Objective response: Seems like you are very disappointed in the results of this project.

Level 3: Intuitive Listening

Intuitive listening is the highest level of listening and is a skill that great leaders have. Intuitive listening is certainly listening to the speaker but also has a broader focus beyond the words spoken. At this level, you are hearing what is being said and also what is *not* being said. You are paying attention to things like body language, tone of voice (or changes in tone of voice), pauses, and speed of voice. You can hear what is most important and what isn't. At this level, you can more deeply understand the speaker and engage with them in a more meaningful way.

Intuitively listening to someone can have a profound effect. The speaker feels truly heard, valued, appreciated, and important. They are more likely to trust you and to listen carefully to your feedback and responses. Intuitive listening also sets you up to better serve the individual, your team, and your organization (or family members or friends) and helps to drive for more success for all.

> **Example:** I'm really upset about the feedback we got from the client on this project.
>
> Intuitive response: While the feedback certainly doesn't reflect our effort on the project, it seems like you're concerned over this and what it might suggest in the longer term.

Guess what? You're human, and humans will inherently listen at all three levels at one point or another. The ability to recognize how much you are listening and then move yourself to the next level over time will demonstrate your leadership success and will directly impact your ability to influence others. Being a great listener helps build relationships, increase buy-in, address conflict, and allows you to customize your approach and response to get the best results for all involved.

Communicating Effectively to Influence Others

Communication is an all-day everyday kind of thing. Communication comes in all shapes and sizes, including verbal, nonverbal, visual, and written formats. All of what is said, unsaid, or written will impact your ability to influence the people around you. It will impact your ability to make connections and engage with people to get them to complete a task, mission, or journey.

TYPES OF COMMUNICATION
AND WAYS TO USE THEM

Verbal
- Use a strong, confident speaking voice.
- Use active listening.
- Avoid filler words.
- Avoid industry jargon when appropriate.

Nonverbal
- Notice how your emotions feel physically.
- Be intentional about your nonverbal communications.
- Mimic nonverbal communications you find effective.

Visual
- Ask others before including visuals.
- Consider your audience.
- Only use visuals if they add value.
- Make them clear and easy-to-understand.

Verbal
- Strive for simplicity.
- Don't rely on tone.
- Take time to review your written communications.
- Keep a file of writing you find effective or enjoyable.

Provided by Indeed

While there are four types of communication, for the sake of your ability to influence others, let's discuss nonverbal, verbal, and written communication.

Nonverbal communication

Managing nonverbal communication takes awareness, focus, and intent. No matter how hard you try to hold in your emotions, the people around you generally see and feel them, especially the negative ones. This means your facial expressions, the way you sit, what you do with your hands and arms, and even micro expressions, which are the hardest to manage and the easiest to miss when trying to navigate your communication skills.

To be an effective nonverbal communicator, you have to be aware of your energy, which includes your thoughts, feelings, and actions. The more aware you are of those things, the more choices you have in how you want to show up and better communicate.

When you are feeling frustrated or let down, consider what that might mean nonverbally. When frustrated, your shoulders may tense up, you may have a furrowed brow, your arms may be crossed, or your breathing speed may increase. When you're feeling let down, those same shoulders may droop, you may have a frown on your face, your gaze could be down to avoid eye contact, or you may even lean back in your chair or shift your chair away to create more space between you and the one you are disappointed in.

Regardless of your emotions and thoughts, your body will have some kind of reaction. It may be the smile or quiver in your voice or how you engage with the audience. Just as your body is your biggest sensor of what is working and what isn't, it can be a quick tell for the people around you.

Your energy introduces you before
you even speak.
— Unknown

Recognize that what you are feeling gives you awareness, and with that awareness, you have a choice in trying to improve your mood, meet the audience where they are, or even express your vulnerability and needs in the moment. Regardless of what you choose to do with the awareness, you have that choice and can shift to make a win-win for those around you.

One last fun fact about nonverbal communication is from Albert Mehrabian, a researcher of body language. He says that when you consider your ability to influence an individual or an audience, body language makes up 55% of what the audience will take away, intentionally or not.

Verbal Communication

Continuing with that statistic, verbal communication makes up the other 45%. This is, however, split, with only 7% being the actual word choices and 38% being your voice.

It's the proverbial saying, *It is not what you say, it is how you say it*, that counts most. Your voice includes the tone, volume, and inflection you use to share your message. The same way that nonverbal communication is influenced by emotions, thoughts, and actions, so is your voice. People can sense your stress, fear, and anger. Your tone shifts up or down, the speed at which you speak increases or decreases, and the inflection you use reflects your emotions, thoughts, and actions.

As a leader, you will regularly communicate with partners, coworkers, and team members. Awareness of your energy is key, and conscious management of your voice will allow you to be a more effective communicator—and a great leader. Being aware of others' energy will also help you consciously manage your verbal communication skills and demonstrate emotional intelligence.

Awareness of voice and verbal communication is particularly important during constructive feedback situations when you may be nervous or tense. It is important to be aware of what you want to say and how you want to say it in advance, but you should also be flexible and understanding of the individual you are communicating with.

Here are a few tips to consider when delivering constructive feedback or difficult news.

Assess the Situation	Consider the Environment	Give the Actual Feedback
How does this individual best receive feedback? Assess where they are emotionally, physically, and psychologically before delivering the information. What are the benefits of this feedback to the person making that change (what is the win-win)? Is this feedback truly about improvement, or is there bias?	Prepare the recipient for what's about to be said. It never hurts to say, "I need to tell you something that may be hard for you to hear." Choose a location that is confidential. Provide time and space for the recipient to clearly understand the next steps. Give the recipient the opportunity to respond. Listen to what they have to say.	Explain why you are sharing this and what you are willing to do to help the person learn from it. Frame the conversation with the outcome in mind. Share what you think is working and then ask them what they think is and isn't working. Focus on the facts and the issue or behavior at hand; the things that can be fixed and learned from.

Put yourself in their shoes to understand perspective, have empathy, and determine the best way forward.	Pay close attention to your word choice, tone, and body language to reflect that you're coming from a place of care and development.	Refrain from resorting to accusations or a derogatory tone and comments. Highlight opportunities for growth over faults. Give specific examples to help them see/understand. Know when to get to the point. You don't need to sandwich constructive feedback between two positives.

Written Communication

Let's not forget about the actual words—that 7% of the communication formula, according to Albert Mehrabian. While 7% can feel insignificant, the actual words that we use and how we place them together are critical to effective communication and should be intentional.

Your word choice expresses to others how intelligent you are, how much you understand the subject matter, and how much you know your audience. While this is not a grammar lesson, your word selection says a lot about you and the perspective you have on the situation.

Word choice also reflects your energy and emotions, whether you intend it to or not.

To ensure that you are choosing the right words and expressing your tone properly, when experiencing heightened emotions (especially negative ones), I encourage you to consider the following when emailing or using written communication:

- Take a beat before responding (up to 24 hours for the really difficult or emotional ones, if needed).
- Write a draft and come back to it.
- Read your draft out loud to consider both flow and tone.
- Put yourself in the shoes of the reader before sending— will they read it the way that you intend?
- Ask a trusted friend or colleague to read it and provide an alternative perspective.
- Assess whether you even need to respond. (If it's a group email, for example, others may jump in, too.)
- If the email or text takes more than a few back-and-forths to gain clarity, pick up the phone or schedule a meeting to discuss, minimizing frustration and lost time.
- Be concise and consider bullet points or bold font to highlight the key takeaways (what is commonly called snackable content).
- Avoid slang and acronyms.
- Avoid passive aggressive language like "as we discussed" and "based on our previous meeting."
- Consider your closing as your way of ending on the right tone (e.g., thank you versus best).

Influence Creates Buy-In

Creating buy-in is brass tacks for influence and is a result of effective listening and communication. Before you can influence others, they need to be on board with what you're trying to do. This requires emotional intelligence, intention and focus, and identification of the win-win, or the *why*. It requires all the communication and listening skills—the listening skills especially—that lead to influence. This creates movement; influence in action.

---

*Leadership is the art of getting someone else to do something you want done because he **wants** to do it.*
— Dwight D. Eisenshower

When people are bought in, they feel part of the solution and connected to the outcomes, so they work harder (and better). More importantly, they get greater satisfaction from the work, resulting in loyalty, retention, and overall well-being. Buy-in becomes enthusiasm when you tap into people's values, benefits for them, and the win-win for why we're doing this.

---

buy-in

\ 'bī-ˌin \

Noun

plural buy-ins

Acceptance of and willingness to actively support and participate in something

---

So, how do you get the buy-in needed to influence your team toward change?

First things first, you have to know who you are trying to influence and why. How are they motivated? What are their intrinsic values? How do they want to grow or be challenged? The more that you understand your audience, the easier it will be for you to influence them toward positive action and gain that necessary buy-in.

As you learn about your team, it's important to know where they are in the buy-in process and where you want them to go (and of course, why). To do this, you not only need to have that awareness of your team, but you also need to assess the advantages and disadvantages of the initiative that you want to get them on board with. This means looking at the situation, the individual, the team, the business, and your own needs. This doesn't have to take long, but it does need to happen so you can know the benefits for others and can fully believe it yourself. This will also help you not only have the vision for the initiative in mind but also formulate a strategic plan for how to achieve it.

Buy-in Process

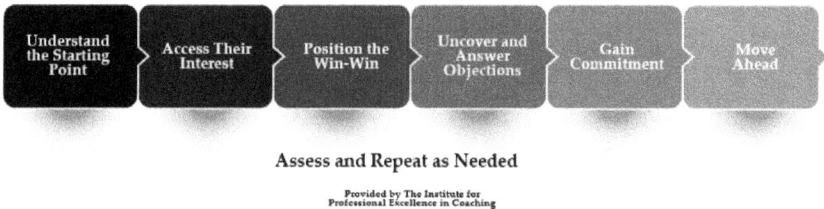

Assess and Repeat as Needed

Provided by The Institute for
Professional Excellence in Coaching

This diagram illustrates the steps in getting buy-in. Let's dig into it a bit more so you can put it into action.

1. Understand the starting point

Ask open-ended questions to build the relationship, understand where the person is coming from, and identify things that impact their buy-in, such as skills and abilities, workload, intrinsic values, and their perspective on the topic or issue. Ask questions that start with who, what, when, where, or even "tell me about..."

I recommend staying away from *why* at this point to avoid defensive feelings and responses.

Going beyond just yes-or-no, one-word answers will not only give you great insights about where the person is, but this will help you understand how best to influence them. It also starts the process for the team or individual to feel that they are part of the process, beginning to create buy-in and holding ownership of the end result.

2. Assess interest

To build upon the starting point of where they're coming from and qualify their buy-in, probe further about their interests and discuss potential involvement in the task. Ask questions like: What do you believe needs to happen to solve this problem? What does a project like this need to be successful? How would you like to be involved in this initiative?

This will help you gauge how invested they are in the initiative or task at hand and help you truly understand their motivations and possible obstacles or objections.

3. Position the win-win

Now that you know where they are and how interested they are (or are not) in the task, you can start to position the project and its benefits to them accordingly. This is the heart of buy-in. Knowing what's important to them and what hesitations they have will allow you to build your case.

Begin describing the initiative or task, weaving in the why and how it relates back to what this person just shared with you. Note: This does not mean making up benefits to gain buy-in; it's about understanding how this work or initiative will benefit those you want to get on board and effectively messaging it to them.

4. Uncover and answer objections

Pause and ask what questions they have. Then ask questions about what challenges or concerns they have, how much they understand, and what excites them about the task, etc.

As the conversation continues, you will learn how much they understand and where their energy is (or isn't), so you can help to remove obstacles and barriers. Continue the conversation to ensure they understand your vision, feel connected to the results, and know why it is important for them and the business.

5. Gain commitment

Outline the initiative, roles and responsibilities, timelines, and expectations and ask for their commitment in advancing the task at hand. If concerns arise, work collaboratively to solve them and reinforce a culture of empowerment and co-creation.

Whether you gain commitment individually or in a group setting, this ensures that each team member understands the assignment and is enthusiastic about how it will lead to greater outcomes.

6. Move ahead

Close the conversation (for now). Confirm understanding and enthusiasm. Ask what you can do to support and help along the way. Agree to next steps and commitments for all. Reinforce the win-win and your personal enthusiasm for the task at hand.

7. Assess and repeat as needed

Circle back throughout the project or initiative to ensure continued buy-in and influence. Identify new roadblocks or obstacles that you can help to remove. And, of course, celebrate all the wins along the way.

Pause for Reflection

Please take a few moments to reflect on what influence means to you.

- How are you influencing people around you today?
- Are you making a positive or negative impact?
- What type of listening are you practicing?
- How well are you communicating (verbally, nonverbally, word choices)?
- How much buy-in do you have in any given task?

Review your Leadership reDEFYned statement. Consider what you've learned about Principle 2: Influence that will need to be applied to bring your leadership vision to life.

CHAPTER 10

LEADERSHIP REDEFYNED™ PRINCIPLE 3: INSPIRE GREATNESS

The final fundamental principle of great leadership is the ability to inspire. It is one thing to influence others toward positive action, but it's a whole other thing to add "pep to their step" or more energy by inspiring them. Inspiration is giving people energy, motivation, and excitement to join you on this great ride. Inspiration is your ability to move attitudes from a place of dread or thoughts of "have to" into a place of enthusiasm.

Once you've influenced people and have buy-in, inspiration taps into and ignites their values, giving them a sense of purpose. Being able to inspire allows you to lift up the team and get them on board with the goals and objectives that you have, including projects, strategic vision, and overall loyalty to your organization and the work you do.

Great leaders don't set out to be a leader...
they set out to make a difference. It's never about
the role - always about the goal.
— Lisa Haisha

Successful leaders focus on *what to say* and *what others need* to influence people to take action. Great leaders focus on *how they can 'be"* to inspire those around them to not only accomplish a task, develop a vision, and create a powerful team, but to do it with passion and fervor for optimized results. Being an inspiring leader means that you are fully engaged (with that "choose to" attitude). It enables you to facilitate strong and enthusiastic connections between the individual and the task at hand so they care at a deeper level and their creative and innovative juices flow without much effort.

Being an inspirational leader not only drives results, but it also creates trust and loyalty (which results in greater retention), attracting others to be a part of the same mission. This transforms your team into one full of opportunities and possibilities.

As a quick reminder, your emotions, thoughts, and feelings are sensed by everyone around you, at all times, whether you intend for them to be known or not. Your energy will either attract or repel people.

As a younger leader, I had a reputation for delivering great work and setting high expectations for my team. For some, those high expectations were motivating and inspiring because they wanted to meet the challenge, grow, and create their best possible work. But those high expectations turned off others because they felt unattainable. This shut them down from considering possibilities or opportunities in front of them. During a heart-to-heart with one of my employees, he bravely informed me about how my leadership style was received by the team, both the motivating and the not-so-motivating parts.

Over time, I adjusted my approach and messaging, so it resonated better with my team and therefore increased my influence. I shifted my focus to the positive intent of the work, the benefit of completing the work, and the growth potential around it. That higher, more positive energy attracted individuals to want to be on my team, commit to the work, and grow their careers with me.

When you have that positive focus and intent and communicate what's in it for them, your team will usually be successful. Why? Because this approach, overall outlook, and buy-in from the team will make up for any differences (or gaps) and add enthusiasm for the challenge at hand.

Being an Inspirational Leader is the Epitome of Follow the Leader

By embracing a *follow the leader* attitude, you are being positive, optimistic, and enthusiastic about opportunities; honest about challenges; and transparent and clear about what's in it for yourself and for others. You are willing to jump in (remember efficacy) or stand back (empowerment). You are willing to flex and adapt as needed. You celebrate all the small and big wins along the way.

Words may inspire but only action creates change.
— Simon Sinek

Being a leader means that you are not just being observed, but also emulated, so you need to be fully aware of your energy and attitude. In other words, how you approach any given situation or activity will determine the outcome from the very beginning. Negativity, stress, or frustration will unintentionally sabotage the results; however, optimism, a focus on opportunities for growth and improvement, and a connection to the task (and the team) will enable greater success.

Remember: Awareness is key. The more you recognize and embrace your thoughts, feelings, and actions (or inactions), the greater the choice in your leadership.

Awareness + Choice = *Intentional* Leadership

As in all parts of this book, it is important to be aware of how you are showing up and managing any negative energy so you can attract the people and the results you need. Small changes within you can motivate and inspire everyone around you, and therefore, everyone will win.

Layered on this, social awareness allows you to shift and adapt your approach to help everyone remain positive and optimistic. The more people feel that energy, the more attracted to it they will be, and the more they will want to be part of this great opportunity. They will also feel better, carrying that positive outlook forward for the people around them.

But You Are Human, too

Let's be real here. There will be times when you aren't feeling positive and optimistic. There will be times when you are frustrated and struggle to be excited about a difficult challenge. There will be times when you have low energy and are exhausted, when you're burnt out and don't see the win-win. This is all natural and normal. You are human.

I am not suggesting that you mask those feelings or behave in a Pollyanna sort of way. This is where vulnerability and honesty come into play, and leaning on the team around you can be a great source of strength and inspiration. By confessing to others that you are feeling frustrated or scared or simply that you're having a hard time, you can not only get the help and support you need, but you open the doors for them to be open and honest with you. This deeper connection, this human connection, will only enhance your relationships with your team and inspire greater work and commitment for the long haul.

A leader, first and foremost, is human. Only when we have the strength to show our vulnerability can we truly lead.
— Simon Sinek

Being open about your positive and negative thoughts with your team members, clients, peers, and social circles will open the door for you to know where they stand, too. The more you know about yourself and others, the greater your ability to meet them where they are, create buy-in, and shift them (and potentially yourself) to greater engagement and greater outcomes.

Inspiration Can Create Buy-in at Scale

As you connect the dots about all the things I've covered in this book, let's revisit buy-in and its relationship to inspiration. Sitting down with *every* employee to get buy-in on *every* ask is overwhelming and may seem unreasonable. This is right—and wrong. The buy-in process is crucial and necessary. If your team is not bought in, the results will be lackluster.

This is where intention and *following the leader* come into play. As you lead your team, there will be times for deeper conversation and times when the buy-in chat is not necessary. Knowing where your team is and empowering them will create a cycle of buy-in that becomes natural, organic, and systematic. As you establish your abilities to inspire, your team will naturally stay on board as long as you are. Long story short: The more you do it, the less you need to.

Success begins with belief and ends with doubt.
— Larina Kase

To Inspire is to Know

To inspire anyone, we must know who they are, what motivates them, how they want to grow, etc. This approach taps into the top tier levels of Maslow's Hierarchy of Needs and supports individuals to have a sense of belonging, to feel respected and valued, to feel that they are growing and becoming better today than they were yesterday.

Maslow's Hierarchy of Needs

Self-actualization
Desire to become the most that one can be

Esteem
Respect, self-esteem, status, recognition, strength, freedom

Love and Belonging
Friendship, intimacy, family, sense of connection

Safety Needs
Personal security, employment, resources, health, property

Psychological Needs
Air, water, food, shelter, sleep, clothing

As a leader, you can effectively inspire the people around you by honoring who they are as a human beings and ensuring that the way you lead allows them to reach the highest levels of actualization. While this may sound lofty, I promise you it isn't. It's a people-first mentality, and by treating others how you'd want to be treated (and seeking to understand how that is working), the inspiration will follow. It's not a complex proposition.

Success isn't just about what you accomplish in your life; it's about what you inspire others to do.
— Unknown

Here is a step-by-step approach to help you inspire your team, create buy-in, and motivate them to grow and achieve more than they ever thought possible:

- **Communicate.** Create a why-based story or message about the need for the strategy, process, project, goal, objective, or task.

- **Create the vision.** Focus on the end result in a clear and concise way that anyone can digest and get on board with. Share the vision broadly and seek feedback along the way. Focus on what's in it for them, or win-win.

- **Develop the plan.** Create a roadmap to guide the initiative and continue to collect feedback to create more buy-in. Adjust as needed.

- **Ensure everyone knows their role**. Define each person's role and responsibility as a contribution to the initiative.

- **Empower.** Don't just delegate the work to others, but actually let them do it. Step out of the way and allow them to make mistakes or fail fast so they can learn and develop. As Winston Churchill said, "Success is not final. Failure is not fatal."

- **Promote creativity and innovation.** Continue to inspire others by giving permission to think outside the box.

- **Reinforce teamwork.** Bring the team together for brainstorming sessions to continue inspiring and offering opportunities for optimization. Ensure everyone feels part of the process and is committed to their part.

- **Role model.** Be effective and do anything you'd ask others to do.

- **Monitor progress.** Develop checkpoints with measurable targets and accountability systems with the team.

- **Have an open-door policy.** Be open to individual and team conversations, and be flexible in updating the vision, plan, or roles.

- **Commitment.** Demonstrate your commitment and determination to the initiative. Others will follow.

- **Achievement.** Recognize key milestones and actions along the way.

- **Celebrate.** Reward individuals and the team on interim achievements and celebrate the end result in a meaningful way.

- **Learn.** Host a retrospective to learn what worked, what didn't, and what lessons to apply to the next project or initiative.

Pause for Reflection

Please take a few moments to reflect on what inspiring others means to you.

- How are you managing your own personal energy and attitude?
- How well do you understand where your team is today, and what motivates them?
- How often are you giving tasks vs co-creating tasks?
- How can you better inspire those around you?

Review your Leadership reDEFYned statement. Consider what you've learned about Principle 3: Inspiration, that will need to be applied to bring your leadership vision to life.

CHAPTER 11

THE RIPPLE EFFECT

A few years ago, I had the privilege of attending the TEDWomen conference. There I watched a presentation by Avery Bang, then the CEO of Bridges to Prosperity, that significantly impacted my perspective on leadership. Avery's presentation was called "Building Bridges and Connecting Communities," and shared how a single bridge could have a massive impact on hundreds of thousands of lives, enabling better health and well-being, connectivity, and growth for the entire community. This single bridge creates a ripple effect, impacting anyone in the surrounding area. The concept of one small thing making a bigger difference than we think possible holds true to our everyday lives, in every way. This concept especially holds true for a single leader having an impact on hundreds of thousands of lives.

This might seem like a stretch, when one leader oversees a team of 10 or an office of 200 or a company of 1,000 people. How does that equate to hundreds of thousands of people?

Just as ripples spread out when a single pebble is dropped into water, the actions of individuals can have far-reaching effects.
— Dalai Lama

A Ripple on the Water

One small drop of water cascades out to create small waves, impacting even the far surrounding parts of that body of water, both on and below the surface. The same applies to leadership; the impact that one leader can have not just on the people they lead, but on their team's team, their team's family, their team's friends, and so many more.

That one drop of water creates a cascade of movement. It creates waves. It shifts both the surface of the body of water and what's beneath. The same holds true for the impact of leadership. One small act can make a significant difference. One act of kindness can make one person smile, which helps the next person they encounter smile, and so on. One moment of frustration and anger can demoralize someone else, creating a toxic energy that moves from one person to the next.

In fact, those negative moments are far more significant than the positive ones. As humans, we tend to focus on unpleasant things or what is missing and needs fixing. It is our natural tendency for survival. We give greater weight and importance to the things that feel bad because subconsciously, we don't like feeling that way, and when we focus on it, we intend to fix it. But let's be honest, it's not always an easy fix, and a single negative moment can create a downward spiral that is very difficult to shift out of.

Think about the people that you come into contact with on a daily basis. Let's say you work with a team of 10 people regularly. Every one of those 10 people is directly impacted by your leadership and how you show up. Now, each of those 10 people works with another 5 people and go home to their families of 3 each too. So now your reach is not just 10 people, but it's 80 people. Just like that, in one day, you've either made a positive impact on 80 people or you've made a negative impact on 80 people. However, the ripple doesn't stop there; say each of those 80 people comes into contact with three more people throughout the course of their evening. So now your reach of 80 is 240 people. You get the idea here; you are making a significant difference in the world around you, whether you are trying to or not. This is where intentional leadership and your ability to live your Leadership reDEFYned™ statement matter most.

Blows Your Mind a Little, Right?

What kind of impact do you want your ripple effect to have?

Think about how you show up every day. Who are you influencing (or inspiring) and in what way? How do they react to and/or are impacted by your leadership approach? And how do those people then react and influence all of the other people in their lives? And so on and so on and so on.

While it can be easy to get caught up in this rabbit hole, let's consider the opportunities that it presents:

- The opportunity to create positive change
- The opportunity to inspire, motivate, and energize
- The opportunity to spread happiness and joy
- The opportunity to create lasting satisfaction (and therefore success)

Not just to one person, but to hundreds of thousands of others in the world around us.

This is your choice every day, in every situation, in every moment. We've talked a lot about intentional leadership (awareness plus choice), so the more you know, the more you can make that positive impact.

Let your leadership be the ripple of change.

> **Pause for Reflection**
>
> Imagine a day in the future, at the end of your life, as you are preparing to say goodbye to everyone around you. As you look back on your life, what do you want to be known for? What are you most proud of? What do you want people to say about you as they reflect on the impact that you've made?

CHAPTER 12

WHAT DOES THIS MEAN TO YOU?

A t the end of the day, what is in this book is only important for you if you can genuinely engage with these concepts and bring them to life. So, let's take a minute to recap what you've learned thus far.

Leadership reDEFYned™ is the belief that we are all leaders. Period. By knowing and honoring your authentic self, you are not only able to be true to who you are and who you want to be, but you will be more successful as a leader than trying to force yourself into a mold that is simply not who you are. This is intentional leadership, or the connection to yourself and your competitive advantage. That, combined with the three principles of leadership (efficacy, influence, and inspiration), will move you from having the potential to be a *good* leader to being a *great* leader.

Intentional Leadership x Three Principles of Leadership
= Great Leadership

Authenticity is the alignment of head, mouth, heart, and feet - thinking, saying, feeling, and doing the same thing - consistently. This builds trust, and followers love leaders they can trust.
— Lance Secretan

Together we have spent time understanding leadership theories, principles of greatness, and fundamental personal offerings. You have taken the time for personal reflection, not only to understand who you are, but also to determine who you want to be. You've had time to think through what matters most to you and what kind of leader you want to be.

While I'd love to keep sharing how-tos and points for consideration, the most important thing is that you know what we've covered so far means for your leadership and your future.

ReDEFYning your leadership is a process. By applying your full self, your vision for your future self, and these base principles to your leadership approach and life, *you can be a powerhouse leader and make a significant impact on the world around you.* You can rise to whatever level you want, you have the capability to feel satisfied and fulfilled in what you do, and you can live the life you truly want. After all, leadership is not just a work thing.

If you haven't taken the time to reflect on who you are and who you want to be, please stop reading here and go back to Chapter 6. If you haven't assessed how to integrate the three principles of leadership into your life, go back to Chapters 8, 9, and 10.

Do not proceed until you have answered those key questions. You need to put in the work for your leadership reDEFYned before you can apply it to your world and step into that next great version of the leader you already are.

—————————Stop here unless you're *really* ready —————————

Because you are still reading (or have just come back from more reflection), I know the work and self-reflection that you have put in have given you an idea of who you today are as a leader, who you want to be, and some key takeaways about the three principles of leadership. You have enough information now to truly begin to reDEFYne leadership and to make a meaningful difference in your approach and to the community around you.

Let's Celebrate!!!

Congratulations on taking your desire to be a great leader to heart and embracing not only who you are today, but also the potential you have to impact on those around you. Being *you* is something that only *you* can do. No one else. No one can add the same value that you can. No one can contribute like you can. No one can deliver, influence, or inspire like you do. You are the most amazing *you*.

Most people chase success at work, thinking that will make them happy. The truth is that happiness at work will make you successful.
— Alexander Kjerulf

Success isn't the key to happiness.
Happiness is the key to success.
— Albert Schweitzer

And the more you believe in yourself, the more satisfaction and joy you will have in life. The more satisfaction and joy you have in life, the greater success you'll achieve.

Most people get that equation backwards. So let me repeat it. *Success does not equal satisfaction. Satisfaction equals success.*

Leadership reDEFYned™ is your pathway to satisfaction and success. It was created to empower you, inspire you, and give you a roadmap for becoming the best version of yourself. And more than that, it was created so that you can make a ripple effect of positive change all around you.

CHAPTER 13

PUTTING YOUR LEADERSHIP REDEFYNED™ STATEMENT (OR LEADERSHIP VISION) INTO PRACTICE

The only constant in life is change.
—Heraclitus

This phrase is totally accurate and a great reminder that we are living, growing creatures who will not be stagnant until we take our last breath. This is true both physically and psychologically. While some may work harder than others to change or grow, we can't help but *always* move forward at some pace.

My hope and dream for this book is that you will walk away a changed person and a more powerful leader. That you will see that your gifts and talents are special and unique to you, and by harnessing them, you will lead well. That you will realize you have the power to grow into exactly who you want to be. That you will embrace efficacy, influence, and inspiration to not just lead, but to be a great leader. And that by being a great leader, you will make a positive impact on the world.

You began the Leadership reDEFYned™ journey by mapping your leadership vision and assessing what steps you want to take to continue growing into that role. I had you do this intentionally, so that you could create a vision based on who you are today and what inspires you today. This planted the seed for you to know powerful information about yourself. You learned how to develop basic leadership skills to become a great leader and reflected on what the three principles of leadership mean to you.

Because you are *YOU* and you are *DIFFERENT* from everyone else on the planet, you will read the words, react to the concepts, and take away different points than any other person reading this book. *What stands out to you is what you need the most right now.*

Know that your leadership vision will change over time. The more you grow and adapt as a great leader, the more you will realize about yourself and the future leader you want to be. You will adjust your vision based on this and on the things you observe and experience that inspire you.

Your leadership vision is fluid and should be revisited regularly, at least every few years, but most importantly when you have a significant milestone in your life, a new job, a promotion, movement within your team, growth or loss in the business or personally with family and friends, a shift in desires as you mature and age, and so on.

At this time, I would like you to revisit your leadership vision statement, incorporating your new insights into leadership and yourself. Return to the end of Chapter 6 and see what you want to shift and evolve. What stands out to you today based on the growth you have experienced while learning to reDEFYne leadership? Revise your vision so it represents your gifts and aspirations for today and the future.

The following questions are designed to help you craft that final vision, assess what is working and what is a growth opportunity, and begin to formulate an action plan to help you embrace the greatness within and grow into exactly who you want to be.

- What does *good* look like (i.e., what does this leadership vision look like when you've achieved it?)
- What is missing that you need to be the leader you want to be in the future?

Congratulations! You have just identified the information you need to create goals that align with your leadership vision. I know that goals can be a very ambiguous word and one that often elicits sighs and other not so fun feelings. But goals are actually really important to your success and to becoming the most successful version of yourself.

Goals are the object of a person's ambition or effort. No more, no less. We tend to use the word "goals" as a generic description for an achievement or accomplishment that we are working toward. Goals are often confused with objectives and actions, which are specific targets and steps within a specific goal. Goals can be personal or professional, and they can be about any area in which you want to grow or improve, including wellness, career, finances, and relationships.

Goals often become one of two things: Too big and ambitious to know what to do with them, or something we write down (or think about) and then forget.

All too often, goals fail. Goals fail because they are not in line with your values. They are not directly connected to your authenticity and don't increase your sense of self. Goals fail because they are supersized and intimidating. Goals fail because they are not measurable.

After years of leading people, a very common goal I hear from people is: *To become a better communicator.* Which I would immediately respond to with: *What is a good communicator?* If the goal is too generic, how will you know when it is achieved?

Goals also fail when they are only focused on a specific time period and are not revisited. I was guilty of this when writing my goals for past corporate jobs. You see, these were a requirement to get into the system, usually by the beginning of March. There was a requirement to review them with my boss around July or August. And then again at the end of the year, when doing my self-assessment. And while I had the best of intentions with those goals, they didn't become part of my everyday life, and they were deprioritized with the chaos of the job.

SMART Goals

Specific

Make your goals specific and narrow for more effective planning.

Measureable

Define what evidence will prove you're making progress and reevaluate when necessary.

Attainable

Make sure you can reasonably accomplish your goal within a certain timeframe.

Relevant

Your goals should align with your values and long-term objectives.

Time-based

Set a realistic, ambitious end-date for task prioritization and motivation.

If you're newer to goal setting, here's a popular framework to help ensure you are setting goals you can achieve:

- Create a goal that is **specific** and **measurable** so you know what you're aiming for and can recognize when you've achieved it.

- Goals must be **attainable,** which is achieved by turning them into an action plan to allow for small wins, momentum, and goal refinement.
- Goals must be **relevant** to your values and big-picture objectives (your *why*).
- Goals must be within a set **timeline** so that they can be prioritized around other responsibilities.

If you didn't notice, these are known as SMART goals: specific, measurable, attainable, relevant, and time-based.

But there's one more rule I need to share with you: **The most successful goals are revisited and evaluated on a regular basis.** As you take steps toward these goals, especially the really big ones, you will learn more about what is working and what isn't, and with this, you'll refine what it is you really want. Goals should be living and breathing, but the intent of the refinement isn't to take the easy way out. It is to make sure that you can adapt and adjust to get exactly where you want to be.

Don't believe me? Let me demonstrate why setting goals and creating action plans is important.

Let's look at a case study.
In his book, *What They Don't Teach You at Harvard Business School,* Mark McCormack referenced a famous Harvard Business School study on the benefits of goal setting and action planning. They polled a group of MBA graduate students as they were heading out into the real world with their new degrees. When asked, the class responded as follows:

- 84% had no set goals
- 13% had goals but no definition or action plan
- 3% had both goals and an action plan

The results 10 years later?

- The group with goals (13%) but no plan was making twice the salary that the bulk of their graduating class (the 84% group) was making.
- The group with goals and plans (the 3%) was making 10 times more than the rest of the class.

While success is not always defined by money, this is a great example of how having a vision and a plan makes a difference in your ability to achieve.

Let me caveat this case study with some controversy. If you Google *Harvard Goals Study*, you'll see that there is debate on whether this study happened in the 50s or the 70s, whether it was by Yale or Harvard, or even if it happened at all. I cite it here for you because it is a powerful example of how focus and determination can turn into something very valuable. Rather than debate the scientific merits of any study, there is significant evidence and a common understanding that goal setting and action planning results in greater success.

Start by Setting Goals

Let's start creating some goals for you based on your leadership vision. These goals include the following areas of growth that you've identified in your vision of what great leadership looks like for you. You've spent time already analyzing what obstacles or roadblocks may get in the way. With that in mind, it's time to start writing out your goals and action plan.

---

*A dream written down with a date becomes a **GOAL**.*
*A goal broken down into steps becomes a **PLAN**.*
*A plan backed by **ACTION** makes your dreams come true.*
—Greg Reid

Step 1: Draft your overarching goal(s)

The very first step is for you to crystallize the goal or goals that will enable you to get closer to your Leadership reDEFYned™ statement or leadership vision. As you think about the end goal, consider what you are really willing to commit to so that you can achieve that goal. Is the goal worth the effort? What effort are you really willing to put into achieving this goal? These questions will help you to solidify your direction and align your why further.

Example: If my goal is to run a marathon, I need to ask myself if I am willing to dedicate months of my life and put wear and tear on my body for training.

Step 2: Define and refine your goal(s)

With that clarity, further define (or refine) that draft. Make sure that your goal(s) are clear and specific, including measures of success and a timeline. Make sure that your goal(s) are achievable and resonate with your values and with the authentic person that you are.

Example: My goal is to run the Chicago Marathon in October of next year to help me both get in shape and give me more energy in my daily life.

Step 3: Create your action plan

Your goal(s) will likely have many steps to them, and by having an action plan, you can make progress and build momentum without feeling overwhelmed or unmotivated. Take your goal and consider if there are any key milestones along the way

Example: To train for the marathon, I want to run a 5K, then a 10K, then a half marathon, and then eventually the full marathon, even though there are many steps between each.

For each goal (or milestone), consider what the very first teeny tiny step will be. And what the next step is. And the next. And then next.

Map out the steps you will need to take to get from today to milestone 1, or to the end goal.

Example:

- Step 1: Research training programs
- Step 2: Buy new running shoes
- Step 3: Determine what approximate date you want to do the 5K
- Step 4: Register for a 5K in that time frame
- Step 5: Complete day 1 of training (½ mile jog)
- etc.

I encourage you to write these out and also revisit them as you learn more about the goal and assess what works for you and what doesn't. As you think about these steps, continue to apply the same SMART framework (specific, measurable, attainable, relevant, and time-bound).

Step 4: Seek accountability

The last step is to consider what outside support you need to achieve your goal(s). For some people, setting a goal in their mind is enough, but they are a rare breed. Most of us need accountability to help us do what we have set our minds on doing.

Accountability can show up in different ways:

- Telling a trusted person your goal
- Telling someone your goal and asking them to check in with you from time to time
- Telling someone about your goal and asking them to check in with you if you don't update them by a specific date

- Telling someone about your goal and letting them know the full plan, so that you are in regular contact with someone about the goal

Did you notice the theme? *Tell someone.* Telling someone you are doing this and asking them to hold you accountable for milestones and achievements will keep you on track. The more you vocalize it, the more it becomes reality. Consider what type of accountability is best for you and seek support. Being vulnerable is not a sign of weakness; it is a sign of strength. We are all human and need each other to succeed.

The Institute for Professional Excellence in Coaching (iPEC), where I received my coach training, is a huge proponent of accountability in goal setting. Accountability helps to guarantee success. It also reinforces my personal belief that relationships make the world go around, or in this case, relationships make the goals work!

Goal Setting and Achieving Tips

Setting and achieving goals is critical for the success of literally every person in the world. A goal is the act of pursuing the object of our ambition. It is deciding what we want and then going after it. The ability to set and achieve goals is also a leadership strength directly tied to great leadership and success. The vision, focus, and action allow you to achieve and become the great leader that you want to be.

If you don't go after what you want, you'll never have it. If you don't ask, the answer is always no. If you don't step forward, you're always in the same place.
— Nora Roberts

Great goal setting aligns with your values, motivation, and your why. More importantly, it aligns with your future.

Here are a few additional tips for consideration when working to set and achieve your goals:

- **Make your goal(s) visible.** Write them out, create a vision board, draw them, or create some sort of visual representation that works for you. Find a way to bring them to life and make them a central part of your daily life. This effort activates a different part of your brain to help cement the goals, pushing you out of rational thinking and giving you a regular reminder of what it is that you are aiming for.

- **Feel your goal(s).** Pretend it is the end of the year and you are reflecting on achieving your goal(s). How does it feel? How does it *really* feel? Envisioning the end goal will give you more confidence and belief in your ability to achieve it. Meditate on your goal(s) and imagine a world in which you are that great leader.

- **Consider what might help you—and what might get in the way.** Analyze what you need to be successful and what could get in your way (often your own fear) to proactively enlist the resources and support you need to achieve your goal(s). This could be a class, a coaching program, a mentor who has done what we want to do, or therapy. Know that you don't have to go it alone.

- **Understand your goal(s).** Why do you want to achieve this goal? What motivates you? What is your intent or your why for the goal(s)? This deep understanding will help you internalize the goals and will directly impact your ability and motivation to succeed.

- **Give yourself grace.** Change is the only constant in life, and you only have control over your own actions and reactions. While you may have the best intentions in working toward your goal(s) and action plans, there may be a time when you don't hit a deadline or quite reach a success measurement. Be sure to give yourself grace and forgiveness along the way—and know that tomorrow is a new day. Rather than fester in the *what didn't*, know that each moment is an opportunity to start fresh.

Goals are instrumental to succeeding in anything you do, in Leadership reDEFYned™ and in life in general. Next page is a template that you can use to develop your goal(s). Please take a few moments now to build your goal(s) and takeaways for action. Be sure to create a goal and an action plan for each of the areas of focus you have identified in your leadership vision. Once you have these crafted, it is time to start!

Goal-Setting Template

Goal What is it that you are going to achieve?		Why What does achieving this goal mean for you?
Goal Measurement How do you measure success?	**Key Milestones** What are key components or activities that need to happen to achieve success?	**Commitment** What are you willing to do that is reasonable and realistic to achieve this goal?

Obstacles/Roadblocks
What can potentially get in the way of your success?

Specific Steps What is the very first step?	Specific Measurement How do you measure success?	Attainable (Y/N) Are you able to complete this with what you already have?	Relevant (Y/N) Is it relevant to your values and vision?	Timeline When will you complete this step?	Accountability How do you want to be held accountable to this goal?

CHAPTER 14

LET YOUR LEADERSHIP JOURNEY BEGIN

N ow great leader, here we go. It's time for you to begin this next chapter of your leadership journey and to step into the fullest, greatest version of yourself.

With your leadership reDEFYned statement and leadership vision, belief in yourself, and tools for success outlined in this book, you are ready to begin, if you haven't already. You have the cake ingredients (efficacy, influence, and inspiration), and you have the buttercream frosting (your authentic badass self), and you have the sparkles for decoration too (your leadership vision for the future). It's time to present your cake to the world: your Leadership reDEFYned™.

I share this cake analogy to give you something concrete to relate to. But know that unlike a cake, you are not creating something permanent. You will change and evolve over time, and your proverbial cake will change too. The first cake you make will not be as impressive as the hundredth or the thousandth. While the first cake is probably really good, your future cakes will only be that much better.

And while you're working on achieving and mastering that vision for your great leadership, know that change is not always easy, but it is well worth the effort. In fact, most change is hard, but through difficult times and growing pains, you will actually grow more and grow faster than if you did not have those opportunities in front of you.

There will be days when you are focused and see the impact and results of your leadership directly. And there will be days when you feel as if the world is out to get you and there is no light at the end of the tunnel. As Van Morrison said, "My mama told me there'll be days like this." But through it all, you are still the most unique, amazing version of *you*. You have abilities like no other. You have gifts and talents like no other. Your heart, mind, soul, and body all work together like no one else's. You are especially you, and that is what makes you *great*.

We are not just the leaders of tomorrow. Leadership is not a destination, leadership is a lifetime journey.
— Lazarus Takawira

Every day, you have choice in being the best version of you, and you have the ability to create a ripple effect of change all around you. You can make a great difference in the world when you harness that ability and open the door for your success—and the success of everyone that comes after you. Remind yourself of who you are and who you want to be and take one step every day that embraces both. Your continued focus, intention, and mindfulness will point you in the direction of great leadership, which is not a destination, but a journey.

Know that I am in your corner and rooting for you every day. You are amazing and will succeed in whatever you truly put your mind to. Your leadership will make a difference. And I cannot wait to see it unfold.

Today is the first day of the rest of your great leadership journey. Go forth and reDEFYne your leadership.

ACKNOWLEDGEMENTS

I'd like to take this opportunity to thank my mentors, family, and friends for their support in the creation of Leadership reDEFYned™. Without your support and words of encouragement, I wouldn't be where I am today. I am grateful for all you do with and for me.

I'd like to thank Steve Uliana, Zach Adamerovich, Emmy Beeson, Ann Ritterspach, Mike Clouse, Nicole Johnson-Scales, Julie Breckenfelder, Audrey LaMere, Melanie Foote-Davis, Holleh Vansant, Tim Vansant, Laurel Petty, Marissa Ballesteros, Vicky Yaeger, Audra McIntosh, Dave Coleman, and Becca Berkenstadt for not only supporting me throughout this process, but for helping me to make sure that the message is clear and applicable for all. Thank you to Debra McCraw for your editorial expertise and perspective to make this book as good as it can be. Thank you ALL for helping me to turn this dream into a reality.

I'd especially like to thank my mentor and friend, Robert Mangone, for instilling in me the belief that I have something special to offer. With the words "don't suck" written on a large post-it on my first day of work, he taught me that I actually *can't* suck. Robert gave me opportunities that no one else did and continually supported me, even when I moved on to a new job. Robert has been and is always available when I need him, and I know that will never end. He taught me the fundamentals of great leadership and taught me that being true to who I am— the *whole version* of who I am— is crucial to my success, my ability to lead, and my ability to impact others. For those reasons and more, I am eternally grateful.

I'd like to thank the Institute for Professional Excellence in Coaching and Leslie Picchietti, in particular, for changing my life and teaching me that I can be the most authentic version of myself and still be successful—in fact, I can be even more successful the more aligned that I am to my values and true gifts. Thank you for helping me take the early steps to creating the life that I really want and creating a career where I am blessed with the ability to make a positive difference in the lives of others.

And to everyone who I have been fortunate enough to meet, work with, coach, teach, etc., I thank you for being open to me and for teaching me along the way. I am beyond grateful for all of you and all of the good times, the bad times, and the really ugly times. Every step I have taken with you has brought me to the place that I am today, and I hope that Leadership reDEFYned™ is a reflection of that journey with you.

GLOSSARY

Leadership: Leadership is moving [someone or something] forward. It is moving a project, a group, an individual, or an initiative forward. It is momentum, progress, and action in the purest form; leadership is motivation, inspiration, and adaptation.

Leadership reDEFYned™: Using your competitive advantage—your strengths, talents, experience, and perspective—to move yourself and others forward in a positive direction. It's an opportunity to DEFY the current standards and bring a new perspective and new approach.

Leadership reDEFYned™ Statement: This vision should be a simple mantra that has meaning and influence to you and you alone. It can be a sentence or two, or a few key words, that empower you and remind you of your goals and your focus. The words don't need to be perfect, and they don't need to make sense to anyone but you. They serve as inspiration, direction, alignment, and understanding of self, and they serve as your guiding light to navigate how you lead—and how you successfully reDEFYne leadership.

Intentional Leadership = Awareness + Choice

Public self-awareness: The understanding of how you show up, appear to, or are perceived by others.

Private self-awareness: The ability to know yourself and reflect on your own thoughts, feelings, and actions.

Great Leadership = Intentional Leadership x Three Principles of Leadership

Three principles of leadership:

- **Principle 1:** Be effective
- **Principle 2:** Influence others
- **Principle 3:** Inspire greatness

Efficacy: The ability to produce a desired or intended result. Efficacy is your ability to do what you say you are going to do, when and how you say you are going to do it. It includes productivity, organization, prioritization, and time management.

Productivity: Doing the most valuable work for the sake of the goal, yourself, your team, or your organization. Productivity is loosely half action (what you do) and half mindset (your source of motivation).

Influence: the ability to shift mindsets and alignment in a positive direction through buy-in (not power or authority)

Buy-in: Acceptance of and willingness to actively support and participate in something

Inspiration: elevating the energy, enthusiasm, and excitement to not only enable "things" to be done, but to be done with more pep, fervor, and ultimately greater results.

Emotional intelligence: The balance between self-awareness, social awareness, and the ability to regulate both.

REFERENCES

Acton, A. (2017, November 3). "How To Set Goals (And Why You Should Write Them Down)". *Forbes*. https://www.forbes.com/sites/annabelacton/2017/11/03/how-to-set-goals-and-why-you-should-do-it.

Covey, S. (1989, August 15). *7 Habits of Highly Effective People.* Simon & Schuster.

Duval, S., & Wicklund, R. A. (1972). *A Theory of Objective Self-Awareness.* Academic Press.

Flip The Script Coaching & Consulting LLC. (2022). "Listening skills activity" [image]. LinkedIn. https://www.linkedin.com/posts/flip-the-script-coaching-and-consulting_management-communication-listeningskills-activity-6963192385363206146-WF5d

Greaves, J., & Lencioni, P. M. (2009). *Emotional intelligence 2.0.* TalentSmart.

Kjidekel, M. (2019, November 6). "These Smart Strategies Will Help You Commit to a Long-Term Goal and See It Through". *Thrive Global.* https://thriveglobal.com/stories/long-term-goals-how-to-set-achieve-strategies-tips.

McCormack, M. (1986, June 1). *What They Don't Teach You in the Harvard Business School.* Bantam.

Perry, E. ACC. (2022, September 14). "What is Self-Awareness and How to Develop it". *BetterUp.* https://www.betterup. com/blog/what-is-self-awareness

Eisenhower (2017, February 7). The Eisenhower Matrix: Introduction & 3-Minute Video Tutorial. https://www. eisenhower.me/eisenhower-matrix/

McKinsey & Company (2024). *Women in the Workplace 2023.* https://www.mckinsey.com/featured-insights/ diversity-and-inclusion/women-in-the-workplace.

ABOUT THE AUTHOR

Tami Chapek, PCC, CPC, ELI-MP
CEO | Founder | Professional Leadership Coach

Tami Chapek, the Founder and Head Coach of WeInspireWe®, has over 25 years of corporate experience in team and individual coaching, strategic performance management and operations, as well as communications. Tami is a seasoned leadership and career coach committed to supporting authentic leadership development for all, regardless of title, tenure, age, gender, or any other qualifier.

Tami holds her Professional Certified Coach credentials through the ICF and Certified Professional Coach and is a Master Practitioner for the Energy Leadership Index through the Institute for Professional Excellence (iPEC). Tami is also a Certified Diversity Coach from Out of the Box Coaching and has received numerous awards for her coaching expertise and offerings. In addition, Tami has served organizations such as Google, Novartis, Fifth Third Bank, Delta, MediData, American Electric Power, Uber, Havas, Syneos Health, Taysha Gene Therapies, Medtronic, and more.

In 2017, Tami founded WeInspireWe® based on the belief that everyone is and has the potential to be a great leader. By leaning into individual strengths, wrapped with fundamental leadership principles, anyone can stretch beyond their current level and unleash their true potential, making a transformational impact in the environment around them. Tami believes that most organizations develop leaders to reach the status quo only, but by defying the ordinary, you can unleash true potential. Because of this, Tami developed the Leadership reDEFYned™ platform to ensure success for all individuals who defy traditional leadership standards. Tami empowers her clients to identify their strengths to reach leadership goals, overcome barriers to success, and own their development path and successful futures.

In addition to coaching, Tami also brings real-world leadership and career concepts to life with hands-on leadership development and career advancement training, customized workshops, employee resource group leadership initiatives, as well as motivational keynote speaking engagements. Tami is passionate about serving women and underrepresented groups like LGBTQIA+ and BIPOC communities, providing a keen focus on empowerment and leadership growth offerings to corporations to expand the diversity and inclusion footprint beyond numbers alone.

ABOUT WEINSPIREWE®

WeInspireWe® is a woman-owned, international Executive Leadership and Career Coaching Firm dedicated to reDEFYning leadership standards to cultivate organizational excellence. Our approach revolves around empowering leaders—regardless of position, tenure, demographics, or any other qualifiers— to maximize their inherent capabilities and create true transformation.

We believe that the best way to lead is authentically and traditional development approaches just produce more of "the same" for your team and your business. This just *doesn't work*. Using a cookie-cutter approach to leadership development will continue to hold you, your team, and your organization back.

By reDEFYning the leadership development process, we empower individuals, where they are, focusing on core strengths and values to *drive true transformation*. This supports them to not only become great leaders but to create exponential impact, inspiring a world full of other great leaders and maximizing the potential for all.

We do this by offering the following solutions:

- 1:1 and Group Leadership, Career, and Performance Coaching
- Leadership Development Training
- Inspirational Keynote Presentations

- Job Seeker and Outplacement Support Services
- Strategic Consulting Services

We especially have a passion for supporting underrepresented groups such as women, LGBTQ+, and BIPOC to become greater leaders in the workforce and in their own personal lives. We know that optimized leadership works to enable diverse thought and representation, collaboration, innovation, and ultimately results in greater success for companies and individuals involved.

To learn more:

SHARE YOUR STORY: JOIN THE LEADERSHIP REDEFYNED™ MOVEMENT

Inspired by the authentic leadership journeys within this book?

I believe true leadership is reDEFYned by authenticity. Your unique path to leading with your true self has the power to ignite inspiration in countless others.

If you've discovered and embraced your authentic leadership—experiencing profound personal benefits, creating positive ripple effects, and gaining distinct advantages—we invite you to share your story.

Your journey can inspire the next wave of authentic leaders.

While not every submission will be featured in future editions of this book, every story shared with us will find a platform to inspire through our social media, workshops, speeches, and digital content.

Ready to contribute to a movement?

Tell us how you found your authenticity, its impact, and the advantages it brought.

Submit your story to:

Sincerely,
Tami Chapek

www.ingramcontent.com/pod-product-compliance
Lightning Source LLC
Chambersburg PA
CBHW031122210326
41519CB00047B/4336